# OLD HOUSE
# NEW HOME

RYLAND
PETERS
& SMALL
LONDON NEW YORK

# OLD HOUSE
# NEW HOME

## STYLISH MODERN LIVING IN A PERIOD SETTING

## ROS BYAM SHAW

### with photography by **Christopher Drake**

Senior designer  Paul Tilby
Senior editor  Clare Double
Picture research  Tracy Ogino
Production  Sheila Smith

Art director  Gabriella Le Grazie
Publishing director  Alison Starling

Dedicated to the memory of Dave Eveleigh,
one of nature's gentlemen.

First published in 2005.
This paperback edition published 2009
by Ryland Peters & Small
20–21 Jockey's Fields, London WC1R 4BW
519 Broadway, 5th Floor, New York, NY 10012
www.rylandpeters.com

Text © Ros Byam Shaw 2005, 2009
Design and photographs
© Ryland Peters & Small 2005, 2009

10  9  8  7  6  5  4  3  2  1

ISBN 978-1-84597-825-9

A CIP record for this book is available from the British Library.

The original edition of this book was cataloged as follows:
Library of Congress Cataloging-in-Publication Data
Byam Shaw, Ros.
  Old house new home : stylish modern living in
a period setting / Ros Byam Shaw ; with photography by
Christopher Drake.
    p. cm.
  ISBN 1-84172-798-9
  1.  Interior decoration.  I. Title.
  NK2113.B94 2005
  747--dc22

                                    2004024121

Printed in China

# contents

# our house

*Most books are the result of direct experience, whether the barely disguised autobiography of a first novel or a straightforward travelogue. This book is no exception. For the past two and a half years I have been engaged in the slow, painstaking and sometimes painful restoration of an Elizabethan house. My writing has been variously accompanied by the noises of chipping, hammering, drilling and sawing, and repeatedly interrupted by questions about the height of a basin, the route of a downpipe or the position of a socket.*

Recently we met an architect now living in Denmark who was born here in 1928. She told us about the 'priest's hole', the 'ghost window', once a door, and the horse skeleton found under the kitchen flags when the drains were replaced after an outbreak of diphtheria. And, as our builders move from room to room, stripping off damp lime plaster and laying pipes under old floorboards, more layers of the past have come to light: a blocked-in fireplace, the tiled base of a bath, a window made into a cupboard, a privy

made into a cupboard, a crisp Victorian penny and a china doll's leg lost down a gap by the skirting board/baseboard.

For four hundred and fifty years, this building has been lived in. Babies have been born, children have died, illnesses been survived, meals cooked. Each generation has adapted the house to suit itself, and used the rooms in slightly different ways. Now we are doing the same. The old kitchen, once steamy with hot laundry, is a sitting room, its stone floor softened by rugs. Bedrooms have been conscripted for bathrooms, and an Edwardian loggia converted to make a home office.

### the second-hand home

Our own house has a longer than usual history, but most people live in houses that are at least second- if not third-, fourth- or fifth-hand. Houses do not become obsolete like cars and computers. Good, solidly constructed houses can, and do, survive for generations. Long after we are dead, someone will be eating in our kitchen or sleeping in our bedroom. Or perhaps they will be eating in our bedroom and sleeping in our kitchen, as room uses and internal spaces are continuously modified.

The buildings in this book vary hugely in terms of date and style. There is a 17th-century French farmhouse, a 1930s Antwerp apartment, an East London townhouse, a Connecticut dairy, a 1960s seaside cottage and its riverside Tudor equivalent. Each of these very different buildings has been reorganized and furnished by its current owners, reflecting not only their tastes but also their daily rituals and way of life.

### all change

While the most basic requirements of shelter, security and, more recently, a degree of privacy have altered very little, the last century has seen a huge advance in standards of domestic comfort and hygiene. Central heating, for example, has transformed the way we inhabit a house. When the only source of heat was an open fire, one or at most two downstairs rooms were kept tolerably warm throughout cold winter days. Freezing bedrooms with frost patterns on the window are well within living memory, as is the Monday wash in a copper of boiling water, the toilet in an outdoor hut, the chamber pot under the bed and the tin bath in front of the fire.

As the practicalities of domestic life have changed, so have the demands we make of the different rooms in our house. Machines have shouldered much of the drudgery of housework, but without servants to do the fetching and carrying, the dining room is gradually becoming redundant. Family life is less formal and segregated than it was for our grandparents. Most people prefer to eat and entertain in the

*ABOVE* Neisha Crosland's South London home was once a mews where horses were stabled and grooms slept in rooms above. Extensively damaged by bombs in the Second World War, the site is now a vernal urban oasis, the buildings extended to make a family home set in a landscaped garden.

*RIGHT* This suburban cottage is a rare survivor, dating back to the 16th century when it housed craftsmen working on Hampton Court Palace.

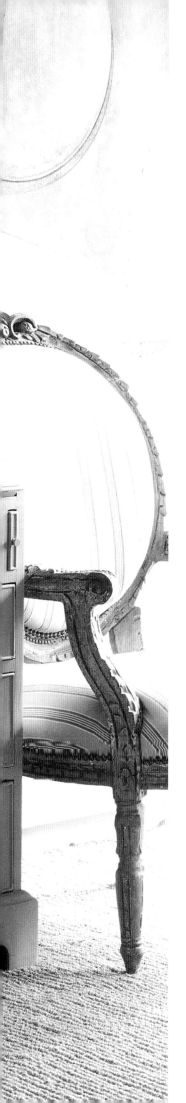

kitchen and, if it is big enough, use it as an extended living room. Home computers are increasingly indispensable, and bundles of electric cabling, not to mention monitors, printers, scanners and speakers, have to be accommodated.

The houses in this book reflect all these new requirements. In some instances radical surgery has been necessary to bring a house up to date, an extension added and internal walls knocked down to make the big open spaces we now prefer. In the case of 'recycled' buildings, the use of space has been changed completely. Other houses have been more gently tweaked into modernity, with new plumbing and wiring, perhaps the addition of a bathroom, or French windows to brighten up a basement designed for servants.

### living with history

Whatever we do to an old building to make it fit us better, we should do with respect both for history and posterity. Most countries have laws to protect the best architecture we have inherited. In some instances these limit the changes that can be made to the exterior of an old house, ensuring for example that original wooden sashes cannot be replaced with plastic. Buildings of particular interest and importance may be further protected, so that their internal features cannot be changed or removed.

Preservation of the original fabric of a house is not simply an aesthetic issue, although old buildings almost always look better with the windows and doors they were built with. Before the ascendancy of steel and concrete, breeze-blocks and plastics, the many components of a house were made by craftsmen whose skills are now either lost or in decline.

### living in style

Old houses make an intriguing setting for contemporary furnishings. In the same way that a well-chosen antique adds a sense of history, texture and depth to the plain cube of a modernist room, a piece of streamlined 21st-century furniture, an eccentric lamp, or a striking abstract painting can freshen an old room like a cool breeze. As the homes on the following pages amply illustrate, an old house need not feel like a museum or a tribute to the fashions of the past. Once we have arranged the spaces to our satisfaction, there is endless scope for making stylish juxtapositions of the old and the new. Then it's just a question of enjoying living in them, which is exactly what I intend to do.

*Ros Byam Shaw*

LEFT  This is the living room of the Tudor cottage pictured on the previous page. Its small rooms and low ceilings, typical of the period, have been opened up at some later date to make spaces more appealing to modern inhabitants. Upstairs, ceilings have been removed so that rooms extend into the roof space and, thanks to the dismantling of the wooden screen that once divided the ground-floor living room from the hall, this room is now big enough to accommodate the ample grandeur of these gilded French chairs.

# PERIOD PIECE

None of the following houses, which date from the 18th to the mid-20th centuries, is in slavish period style. Even Tim Whittaker, who has revived his Georgian range and scraped walls and ceilings back to near-original flaking distemper, has modern plumbing and a full complement of white goods. But each is an example of careful restoration and conservation, and each is furnished and decorated in the spirit of the age in which it was first built, whether the 'Georgian minimalism' of Stephen Pardy's London home or the streamlined luxury of Eric De Queker's 1930s Antwerp apartment.

# cupboard love

*'I strongly feel that houses of this period should have a "below stairs",' declares Stephen Pardy. 'Somewhere you can go to do household jobs like the ironing, or to mend something. Somewhere you can store spare vases and crockery, out of season clothes, things you need but don't use often.'*

Stephen Pardy is a designer with particularly well-developed thoughts on how best to use the limited space in a typical, modest, terraced townhouse. His own dates from 1794 and sits in a quiet London square of similar, but not identical houses, each a mere fourteen feet (four metres) wide, with a couple of steps up to their arched front doors, a basement below pavement level and three floors above. They were built as middle-income family homes. In the 19th century the area fell on hard times and the earliest census to

*BELOW* Furnishings from different periods — 18th century Delft, 19th century William Morris chairs and 20th-century paintings — share a simple, restrained and very English style in the dining area. The room is practical enough for everyday meals, as there is no space for a table in the kitchen.

*ABOVE* The two ground-floor rooms are used as a study at the front and a dining room at the back, next to the small kitchen extension. The alcoves on either side of the chimney breast are ideal for built-in bookshelves. Stephen added folding shutters, their design copied from another house on the street, which had retained its original woodwork.

*LEFT* The wooden fielded panelling wall which separates the entrance hall from the study was one of the few original features to have survived.

mention the house shows nine adult occupants, each probably using single rooms as bedsits.

Today there are only two adults inhabiting the same space and, although none of the rooms is large, the house feels remarkably spacious. This, according to Stephen Pardy, is due to a number of decorating tricks and lots of storage. 'Cupboards are as important as "below stairs" space,' he says. 'We all have so much stuff nowadays it is the only way to make an interior of these proportions work. It's what I call "Georgian minimalism".'

Faced with a house on four floors many people choose to use the bottom floor for their kitchen, the ground floor as reception rooms and the rest

The new woodwork of cupboards and shelves joins seamlessly with the old panelled wall in the study, where the rebate of the fielded panels has been neatly co-opted as a letter rack. Here, as in every room, cupboards store the clutter that would spoil the effect of modest elegance. Even the computer wires are tucked away.

ABOVE Stephen Pardy built this bay
window out from the small 1950s
kitchen extension at the back of the
house. It makes invaluable extra space
for a large Belfast sink, ample wooden
drainers and the dishwasher. The style
is more Arts and Crafts than Georgian,
which seemed appropriate for a part of
the house so obviously a later addition.

as bedrooms and bathrooms. Stephen Pardy thinks this is a mistake.
'When these houses were built, basements like mine were coal holes
and sculleries. I have seen people having subterranean dinner parties
in the worst room in the house. And because families tend to live in
their kitchens, the reception rooms on the floor above become dead
space, bypassed on the way up to the bedrooms and bathrooms.'

His own basement has two rooms, one entirely devoted to shelves
and cupboards, the other kitted out with a reclaimed Belfast sink
and home to the washing machine, tumble drier and boiler. There
is a sturdy work table, a stack of logs for the fires upstairs and a
capacious wine rack. The small kitchen is in a later extension at the
rear of the ground floor, and the original front and back parlours,
linked by a square opening, make a combined study and sitting

*LEFT* The main bedroom is almost filled by the iron bedstead, its head against the wall where there was once a fireplace. In place of bedside tables, there are cupboards and shelves built into the alcoves on either side of the chimney breast. Above the bed is a painting by Craigie Aitchison. The picture light over it works perfectly as an overhead reading light.

*BELOW* Stephen replaced all the shutters in the house and fitted neat, cream roller blinds into the window rebates. These barely show until they are needed to provide shade or privacy. The combination of blinds and shutters is flexible and practical. Shutters are effective insulation from weather and noise, and offer extra security. The lack of curtains frees up wall space and makes the rooms seem spacious and airy.

room at one end and a dining room at the other. The Pardys use the dining room every day, and they often sit in the study in the evening.

On the first floor they use the front room as a drawing room, a retreat one remove from the street with pretty views across the square. Next to it is a spare bedroom and at the back, above the kitchen extension, there is a cloakroom with a large shower. The main bedroom and its bathroom are on the top floor. And everywhere there are cupboards and shelves, fitted into alcoves on either side of the chimney breasts, slotted into landing space on the way up the stairs and even built across the corner in the dining room.

Despite appearances most of the woodwork, including the drawing-room panelling to dado level, is new, as are the windows, which replace 'awful' 1950s casements. According to Stephen, the house was 'grim' when they bought it, with all its period charm knocked out. 'All I have done is repaired what ought to have been there. I have tried to keep the infrastructure in period so that new additions, like the bathrooms, and the kitchen and our contemporary paintings, can be layered on top.' Or hidden in cupboards.

*LEFT and ABOVE* Tim uses the reception room at the back of the raised ground floor as a drawing room, but the original cornice with its moulded hops and grapes, and the traces of Etruscan red paint, indicate that it was originally the dining room. The panelling has been painted with a flat oil paint from Farrow & Ball, the closest modern equivalent to old lead-based paints, but the ceiling with its picturesquely mottled layers of pink and grey distemper was left well alone.

*RIGHT* All the architectural features added to the house have been salvaged from houses of a similar age, like this piece of French panelling over the fireplace in Tim's study.

# one careful owner

*To see professional chef Harvey Cabaniss roast a chicken on a clockwork spit over an open fire in his Georgian kitchen might lead you to believe that he and his partner Tim Whittaker had gone a little too far in their quest for period authenticity.*

*ABOVE* What was once the front parlour is now the main bedroom, presided over by a four-poster hung with William Morris curtains from a castle in the Scottish Borders. The half-glazed door and sash windows, which now divide this room from the drawing room, were found on the street and recycled as internal partitions.

*RIGHT* The zinc bath which sits between the bedroom windows is 19th-century French, bought from a South London salvage yard. One of the advantages of panelling is that pipes can be hidden and the taps fixed to the wall. The wide deal floorboards are original and have been scrubbed for a pale, matt finish that looks far more authentic than varnish.

Look up, however, and you will see an entirely 21st-century recessed spotlight in the ceiling above, and if you were to peer into the two cupboards under the stairs you would find a modern electric oven and a dishwasher. Another cupboard hides a microwave.

Harvey chooses to cook his traditional roasts in a traditional manner and also likes to use a pan stand from IKEA balanced over the fire for a hotplate. Although the house looks as though time has barely touched it since it was built two hundred years ago, it has a full stock of white goods, and it is centrally heated and plumbed, with two bathrooms, plus the luxury of a bath in the main bedroom. The fact that at first glance the 21st century seems barely to intrude is the result of careful restoration coupled with some clever disguise.

Tim Whittaker is Administrator for the Spitalfields Trust, a charity that has rescued dozens of 18th-century London houses from vandalism and ruin. It took an expert eye to recognize the potential of this forlorn architectural gem in distress, on a litter-strewn East London street. When he bought it the house had been used as a sweatshop and cheap clothes emporium since the 1970s. Its plain, late 18th-century façade was disfigured with steel roller shutters, a neon shop sign and an ugly UPVC front door. Inside were suspended ceilings, hardboard partitions, and strip lighting.

This 'post-war grot' was fortunately only skin-deep, an added layer of cheap modernity, which once removed revealed fireplaces,

floorboards, panelling and plaster cornices dating from the house's genteel past, when it was occupied by a mother and her four unmarried children and subsequently by a sea captain. In the mid-19th century the basement had housed a ship chandler. Later there was a linen draper and then a tailor.

The raised ground floor had been opened up to make a single shop space, but underneath modern flooring lay the original deal boards bearing traces of the old room layout. Tim put walls back where they would have been, using a combination of 18th-century

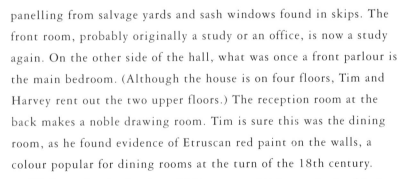

panelling from salvage yards and sash windows found in skips. The front room, probably originally a study or an office, is now a study again. On the other side of the hall, what was once a front parlour is the main bedroom. (Although the house is on four floors, Tim and Harvey rent out the two upper floors.) The reception room at the back makes a noble drawing room. Tim is sure this was the dining room, as he found evidence of Etruscan red paint on the walls, a colour popular for dining rooms at the turn of the 18th century.

While modernity has been hidden, any additions, whether kitchen shutters, panelled walls, internal windows, or a replacement fire grate, have been rescued from other old buildings. Even the radiators are salvaged, reconditioned and given a gunmetal finish, and the bath in the bedroom is 19th-century French. Fortunately for such a purist there was already a 1920s extension at the back, where he put two new bathrooms. But it is as much the things Tim Whittaker has not done that give this house its venerable air of 'pleasant decay'.

It is under- rather than over-restored, stripped back with only the thinnest veil of 21st-century convenience overlaid. Floorboards are scrubbed and all woodwork has been painted in dead flat oil from Farrow & Ball, the nearest available equivalent to old lead paint. He is thinking of removing the recessed ceiling lights in the drawing room. They are just too intrusive.

*FAR LEFT and TOP LEFT* **Tim rebuilt the hob grate in the basement kitchen and installed an adjustable ratten-crook for hanging pans on. Even though there is a microwave and a conventional electric oven hidden in a cupboard, Tim's partner, chef Harvey Cabaniss, often chooses to cook over the fire. In complete contrast, there are recessed ceiling spotlights tucked into the spaces between the beams. The original flagged floor, laid on compacted mud, was taken up and relaid for a more level surface.**

*ABOVE* **A set of shelves with cubby holes and drawers from an old chemist's shop provides useful storage.**

*LEFT* **Another room in the basement, once used as a ship chandler, linen draper and later a tailor's premises. Much of the original woodwork in these rooms has survived, and has been left complete with holes and patches, under rather than over restored.**

*LEFT* The huge double reception room extends into a corner of this purpose-built block. Translucent, white blinds filter the light that floods in from windows on three sides.

*ABOVE* An elongated arch divides the room. Both ends are furnished with low, modern seating including a long sofa by Nathalie van Reeth and grey-flannel-covered seating by Jean de Mulder. Their sleek lines and luxurious, tactile materials have just the right feel for their stylish Deco setting.

# art deco glamour

*Eric De Queker's Antwerp apartment has all the glamour of a 1930s ocean liner, but none of the excess. He bought it from its original owner, an influential and creative Belgian builder who had collaborated on the design of the building with Jean-Michel Frank, himself one of the most highly regarded designers of furnishings and interiors of his day.*

No expense was spared in the fitting out of the rooms; the floors are a golden mosaic of oak parquet, diagonal chequerboard in the hall, modulating to herringbone in the large double living room. There are inlaid borders around the edges. Skirtings/baseboards and

architraves in the hall are in exotic striped zebrano. Elsewhere walls are panelled in unusual oak burr veneer, its striking wavy grain polished the same golden brown as the floors. All the radiators are housed in wood veneer covers and the bathroom retains a splendid double basin and massive roll-top bath in a shade of pale avocado that was doubtless the height of chic at the time. 'Nothing,' says Eric De Queker, 'had been changed. When I first viewed it the apartment contained all its original Art Deco furnishings.'

The furnishings were not for sale. De Queker runs one of Belgium's best-known furniture and interior design companies and decided to furnish the apartment with contemporary pieces rather than seek out replacement furniture of the period. 'In fact the Deco furnishings gave the interior an oppressively old-fashioned feel,' he explains. 'I wanted to find equivalents that were in tune with the 1930s aesthetic of streamlined luxury but create a more modern look and atmosphere.'

Art Deco style was characterized by lavish use of rich materials. Jean-Michel Frank was known for his use of rare woods and veneers, parchment, lacquer and for details in bronze and ivory. Eric has chosen furnishings with long, low profiles, which suit the horizontal emphasis of the rooms. Designs are simple and colours are plain and neutral, ranging from blacks through brown to greys, cream and white. But true to the spirit of Deco, materials are sensuous and tactile: the coffee stool is upholstered in short, silky fur; the rugs are squares of creamy black leather; the safari chairs are a masculine combination of wood and leather; and cushions shimmer in black chenille.

By choosing furnishings that Eric says he 'felt in his heart' were right for the apartment, he has enhanced rather than detracted from its Art Deco style. The only room that has been completely modernized is the kitchen. The apartments were built for owners whose servants lived in separate flats and cooked in a communal kitchen. Times have changed, but the glamour is undimmed.

*ABOVE* Exotic, striped zebrano wood frames the doors in the generous entrance hall. Even the pictures are hung deliberately low to emphasize the long, lean, horizontal aesthetic that is so typically 1930s.

*RIGHT* Eric uses what was once a bedroom as his dining room. The kitchen is tiny, as when the apartments were built residents were served by cooks who worked in communal kitchens elsewhere in the block.

The bed in the main bedroom sits in a recess formed by flanking, original cupboards. Here again, the period woodwork takes on a thoroughly modern look when matched with a simple, contemporary divan, and a striking enlarged photograph of a flower. The walls are painted inky blue, against which the golden brown of the wood almost glows, and the bedside light is an original fitting from Eric De Queker Design.

*LEFT* The main living room is on the third floor and takes advantage of the views across the raised sea defences to the shingle beach and the sea, through floor-to-ceiling windows and a glazed door which opens onto a wide balcony. The stacked horizontals of the wooden Venetian blinds set up a pleasing counterpoint with the vertical lines of the pine tongue-and-groove panelling.

*ABOVE LEFT and RIGHT* Philip Hooper chose to furnish the house in a contemporary version of 1950s style using a mix of vintage pieces and sympathetic contemporary designs. The pair of armchairs are by Robin Day and the daybed opposite them is by Capellini. 'The design of the house is so strong,' he says, 'that it needed strong things in it.'

*BELOW* Unusual and quirky pieces from the 1950s, like this glass-topped desk and bent plywood chair, are now fashionable, desirable and expensive, but when Philip Hooper started collecting them to furnish his 1950s home they were still a minority taste.

# beside the seaside

*Phoebe and Walter Merrick were landowners and fruit farmers in East Sussex in the 1950s. They were also active patrons of the arts with a reputation for avant-garde taste. When they decided to build a beach house on the coast near their home they asked Michael Patrick, then head of the Architectural Association, to design it.*

The brief was for a house where they could have picnics, sleep the night, entertain informally, and where their teenage children could hang out with friends: in short, they wanted a grown-up playhouse. They gave their architect free rein and the result was a small, perfect essay in modernism, a three-storey box balanced on Corbusier style 'pilotis' (slender supporting pillars) and with an asymmetrical arrangement of windows. A panel of black-stained weatherboarding echoes local vernacular architecture and there is an outdoor staircase, which zigzags from the garden to the first floor and up to a long balcony on the top floor.

In 1993 interior designer Philip Hooper, now a Design Director at Colefax & Fowler, bought the house from the family who built it.

He and his partner Alan Fergusson intended
to live there all year round. 'Although it was
extremely cold in winter,' he remembers, 'it
was immediately apparent how clever and well
thought out the design was.' The living room and
kitchen are on the top floor with views of the sea
through floor-to-ceiling windows at the front and
equally attractive views through chest-level
windows on either side, which cunningly skim
above the neighbouring low-level bungalows.

On the floor below are four small bedrooms,
organized like the compact cabins of a boat with
raised beds, each with its own strip of window
and view and with storage beneath. The ground
floor comprised a pod between the pilotis, clad
in blue-painted tongue-and-groove boarding with
an entrance hall and a cloakroom. Owing to the
height of the sea defences, which were built up in
the 1940s, there is no sea view from this level.

The house had barely been changed since it
was finished in the late 1950s. Such was Philip
Hooper's respect for its design that he decided to
keep it as true to its playful, modernist spirit as
possible and only to make the most minimal
structural changes. He even bought some of the
original furnishings, including the dining table,
which is an early design by Terence Conran. 'I felt
that someone else had already done all the work,'
he says. 'It was almost an anti-design project.'

*ABOVE LEFT* **The small open-plan
kitchen is complete with all its original
storage cupboards. Philip Hooper has
reinforced their playful style with his
choice and placing of furnishings; the
Ico Parisi table with its sky-blue
marbleized top, the low-hung picture,
and the lollipop-shaped cactus (right).**

*ABOVE RIGHT* **The house was
originally designed as a fun house. The
only layout change that Philip Hooper
made to turn it into a permanent home
was to install a bigger, more practical
kitchen on the ground floor. Upstairs
is now a secondary 'serving' kitchen,
with fridge, hotplate and sink.**

To make winter more comfortable he installed central heating
using plain, flat-panelled radiators, most of which are hidden
behind furniture. The tongue-and-groove pine panelling which
lines all the walls, its patina intact, was removed and carefully
numbered when pipes were put in so it could be replaced in perfect
order. A Danish wood-burning stove in the top-floor living room
provides a further source of heat and a focus for the room on cold
days. The blue ground-floor pod was doubled in size to make a
second kitchen, more convenient for summer entertaining outside,
and to make space to house the boiler and washing machine.

As for furnishings, Philip and Alan fortunately started collecting
mid-20th-century pieces just before the fashion for them really took
off. 'I wasn't comfortable with most English design of that period,'
Philip explains; 'it just wasn't sexy enough, although we do have a
pair of Robin Day armchairs and a collection of Poole pottery.' Most
of his favourite pieces are Italian or French, like the glass-topped
table by Ico Parisi. To call this 'anti-design' is to underplay Philip
Hooper's skill. The spirit of the house remains intact, but it has
been subtly brought up to date and upgraded for year-round living.

The first-floor bedrooms are as
neat and practical as ships' cabins.
The raised, fitted beds have two
advantages: there is a view of the sea
from pillow level through the raised
strip of window, and there is plenty
of storage space below the beds.

# period piece furniture and lighting

Furnishing a house entirely in period is not only expensive and impractical, but also potentially dull. Rooms filled with items of one particular date and style often have a static, museum-like quality. At their finest, perfect period rooms are beautiful to contemplate, but not generally comfortable to live in. For a house to be a home, rather than a showpiece, period style must be adapted to suit modern tastes and habits. All the houses on the previous pages take the spirit rather than the letter of their period as the cue for their interior design, and all have their full complement of 'mod cons'.

A few pieces of antique or vintage furniture that chime with the date and status of their architectural setting are the key to creating a period atmosphere. One carefully chosen, good-quality antique can be enough to inform the style of a whole room. Finding contemporary pieces to mix happily with antiques means making a visual link between them, whether of style, proportion, colour or material. Finding contemporary lighting to suit houses that were built before electricity also requires careful thought.

BUYING ANTIQUES need not be daunting or expensive. Unusual or rare pieces may fetch a premium but there are plenty of more run-of-the-mill items such as chests of drawers, occasional tables and sideboards, which cost no more than their modern equivalent, and are generally much better made.

BATTERED SECOND-HAND FURNITURE can be revived and smartened up with paint. A matt finish in a drab brown, grey or dark blue can look authentically 18th century.

DON'T BE AFRAID to mix periods of antique furniture. Scale and line are more important for compatibility than the date of a piece.

PRETTY OCCASIONAL CHAIRS can be picked up for under £100, one of the cheapest ways to introduce an antique into a room. Even if too wobbly to sit on, they can be useful in a bedroom for draping clothes.

LOOSE COVERS in plain white give soft furnishings a timeless look, and are reminiscent of the case covers once widely used on chairs and sofas to protect expensive materials from wear and tear and sunshine.

AVOID REPRODUCTION FURNITURE; it invariably looks cheap and nasty because, even if the shape is right, it is impossible to imitate the patina of age with new paint or polish. The exception is sanitary ware.

FITTED CUPBOARDS make the most of limited space and can be given a period feel, whether for a kitchen or a bedroom, with panels and applied mouldings to match original doors.

RECESSED SPOTLIGHTS are suitably discreet but if you want to install a central pendant light, lanterns or chandeliers are more suitable for 18th-century rooms, glass shades for 19th- and early 20th-century interiors. All are widely reproduced.

TABLE LAMPS are more flattering than overhead lights and are easier to find in simple, affordable designs to complement old furniture.

DIMMER SWITCHES allow you to control the level of lighting and recreate the crepuscular gloom of rooms lit by oil lamps or gas.

CANDLELIGHT is the most flattering of all, and a period room is the perfect excuse for it.

# period piece fabric and finishing touches

Fabrics, pictures and ornaments have always been a crucial element of domestic interiors, from the days when tapestries softened and insulated the stone of castle walls and the family plate was displayed on the sideboard as a symbol of wealth and status.

Today, even the most luxurious fabrics, which would once have taken many man or woman hours to create, are machine-made and readily available, whether crewelwork to dress your Tudor bed or silk on silk embroidery to make a cushion for an 18th-century chair. Many fabric houses use archives to inspire their designs, some of which may be direct reproductions, some adaptations of old fabrics.

Once the main building blocks of a room are in place — furniture, lighting and flooring — adding in the pictures, ornaments, rugs and cushions that make it feel like your home is an enjoyable, if potentially time-consuming, process. Slowly collecting things that are the right style or period to suit the architecture of your house can be immensely satisfying. Controlled clutter and even patterned walls are again fashionable after years of pared-down minimalism. A period house can be the perfect setting for them.

**ANTIQUE TEXTILES** are unbeatable for that classy authentic look, bearing in mind that fabrics are fragile and may be too damaged to be practical.

**LENGTHEN THE LIFE**, and if necessary the drop, of a pair of antique curtains with new lining and a contrasting border along the bottom and up the leading edge where they are likely to be most worn.

**VINTAGE FABRICS** from the 1950s and 1960s can sometimes still be found in charity shops and junk shops. Use dress fabric of the period to make cushions.

WHEN CHOOSING NEW FABRICS the enormity of choice can be bewildering. Start by marking pages in decorating books and magazines showing the look you would like to achieve. Your local decorating shop can then point you towards the books of swatches most likely to appeal.

CLUTTER AND PATTERN are coming back into vogue, but just as clutter needs to be controlled, pattern needs to be balanced by areas of plainer colour. Use plain or striped curtains with patterned walls and patterned fabrics against plain backgrounds.

IN A ROOM WITH LIMITED SPACE and pretty windows, a combination of roller blinds and shutters takes up less wall and floor space and is both practical and flexible.

AN ANTIQUE QUILT is a particularly charming disguise for a modern duvet.

COLLECTIONS, whether of 20th-century Poole pottery or 18th-century snuffboxes, often look their best when grouped together rather than dotted around a room.

A FRAME can make or break a picture. Look out for bad pictures in good frames and good pictures in bad frames — you may be able to swap and get a good picture in a good frame.

THE POOR MAN'S PRINT or etching is a photocopy. On good-quality paper and framed in plain black, photocopies are surprisingly convincing.

# URBAN CHIC

It is relatively easy to create a good impression if you stick to a single style when decorating, whether all white Swedish Gustavian or all wood and leather 21st-century modern — the interiors equivalent of always wearing black so you never have to worry about your choice of shoes and handbag. But coming up with a look that is original and intriguing as well as smart and well co-ordinated is more of a challenge. The most sophisticated interiors have always mixed and matched styles and periods, juxtaposing the old with the new, making visual links and striking contrasts. This is the essence of urban chic.

# patchwork palace

*LEFT* The staircase hall is at the centre of the apartment on the lower of the two floors. Doors on either side of the fireplace lead into the dining room and adjoining kitchen. Opposite them, behind the staircase, are the bedroom and bathroom.

*Interior designer Frédéric Méchiche knew exactly what he wanted. His ideal Paris base was a house in one of the old, narrow streets of the Marais, preferably not too far from the Picasso Museum, with a modest, classical interior from the late 18th-century Directoire period. Panelling would create the ideal architectural setting for his ever-changing collection of art and furniture, as long as the rooms were also large and light.*

But, as is so often the case when you imagine something you want, whether an impeccable pair of shoes or a house to suit all your needs, 'the perfect shell', as he calls it, could not be found. Instead of adjusting his ideas and compromising on one or more of his requirements, Frédéric Méchiche set about creating it himself.

He was fortunate to find three adjacent apartments, which could be knocked into one, in one of the prettiest streets in the Marais. Internal divisions were swept away until all that remained was 'a giant hole with four walls', the outer walls of this late 17th-century building. Then began the process of dividing the hole back into rooms. These new spaces were lined with wooden wall panelling, or 'boiseries', salvaged from a Louis XVI postal relay station.

*LEFT, ABOVE AND RIGHT* Despite appearances, the interior architecture of this supremely elegant Paris apartment is completely new to the building. The jigsaw of dismantled panelling, fireplaces and overmantels has been so cleverly put together it looks as though it has always belonged. Even the staircase is new, its graceful sweep designed around an antique metal balustrade. Méchiche is a master of juxtaposing the old with the new, combining the visual interest of contrast with the satisfaction of aesthetic links, for example between the curve of the Castiglione floor lamp and the stairs behind it. The futuristic lounger, *ABOVE*, is by Olivier Mourge.

It was at this point that Méchiche heard that the floor above was also available. Fortunately, so was more of the same panelling. He adapted his plans to make space for a sweeping staircase constructed to his own design around a delicate 18th-century metal balustrade. More panelling was imported to line the walls of the second floor. New flooring was laid upstairs and down in reclaimed oak, worn to a smooth, silvery sheen. The entrance hall and the bathroom were treated to stone paving, also reclaimed and polished by age.

This big, bright apartment now comprises seven rooms. The upper floor is a single open space, with a small gym opening off it and with slim pillars taking the weight once carried by walls. It feels almost like a gallery where pieces of contemporary sculpture, African tribal art, and items of furniture with the presence of sculpture rub stylish shoulders. Downstairs the spacious staircase hall doubles as a library, its walls divided into blocks of shelving, which rise up between the windows and even surround the doors. On this floor there are also a bedroom and a bathroom, a kitchen and a dining room, one opening into the other.

At the top of the stairs is a single, open living space, again lined with a patchwork of old panelling reclaimed from the interior of a late 18th-century postal relay station. Here the juxtapositions continue apace with a meeting of classical giltwood pieces, upholstered in snowy white, and iconic 20th-century furnishings and artworks.

*LEFT* One end of the room opens into a small gym. Having previously lived in an open-plan loft Méchiche was keen to recreate the same openness in this more traditional interior.

The panelling, which arrived in sections comprising tall rectangles surrounded by chunky mouldings, engaged pilasters, and simple, carved friezes, has been skilfully arranged to centre on walls and around doors so that it looks as though it was designed specifically for these rooms and not for a series of offices miles away. In places it has been cut, in others added to. Joins are perfectly disguised by a uniform coat of white paint. Far from a patchwork, these wooden panels serve to link the rooms stylistically and to give the apartment an architectural integrity and sense of history. Furnishings throughout adhere to a strict colour scheme of monochrome black and white, and sepia brown and cream.

Méchiche is pleased with the effect. He describes the process as 'like fitting together the pieces of a puzzle' and says the impression he wanted to create was that he had found the apartment intact and done nothing more than paint it with a 'fresh coat of whitewash'.

Just as he had hoped, the space he has created forms the perfect background for his array of furnishings. These are regularly added to and subtracted from but always comprise the same bold hybrid of dates and styles in the same colour palette, whether a Georges Jacob chair in front of a playful 20th-century sculpture, a group of African masks on a giltwood console, or a pair of plastic laminate tables next to an 18th-century painted settee; pieces from widely varying cultures and periods but united by their elegance.

*ABOVE* The strict colour scheme, which helps the whole apartment and its extraordinary range of contents to cohere, is continued in the bedroom, where bold black and white stripes cut through the cream of walls, bed linen and upholstery.

*LEFT* The bathroom combines the best of all possible worlds. The interior architecture is all reclaimed and of the Directoire period, like the panelling in the rest of the apartment. The marble floor is also reclaimed, with that deep gloss that only comes from the gradual polish of generations of feet. The magnificent bath with its swan's head taps is also an antique. However, the water pressure and the underfloor heating are entirely modern luxuries.

*FAR LEFT* The washbasin has been inset into an elegant marble-topped washstand. Modernity is introduced in the pair of unusual wall lights and the pair of 1970s Perspex and metal chairs on either side of the bath (seen left).

# baby grand

*A first-floor reception room on the Place Vendôme in Paris is a very grand room indeed. The ceilings are sixteen feet (five metres) high and the windows stretch from top to bottom and open onto ornate iron balconies and a view of one of the most beautiful royal plazas in Europe. The layout of the plaza and the façades of the buildings were designed by Jules Hardouin-Mansart, architect of much of the Palace of Versailles. Internally, however, different properties were always arranged according to the tastes of individual landholders. Three hundred years later, the same principle applies. The façades of the separate apartments cannot be altered, while behind the splendid ranks of windows there are as many different styles of accommodation as there are occupants.*

*LEFT* When space is at a premium furnishings must be chosen with particular care. A straight-lined modern sofa in handsome black leather offers a comfortable place to sit and glory in the view of the Place Vendôme, while the pair of antique Chinese chairs can provide extra seating as well as a useful repository for books and cups of coffee.

---

*ABOVE and RIGHT* A small dining table tucks behind the sofa. On its far side a compact kitchen, complete with hob, microwave, fridge and storage, is enclosed in an opaque glass column.

---

This glamorous pied-à-terre is a self-contained portion of a much larger apartment spanning five windows. Locking double doors connect the two, so that one day they can be reunited. The owner rents out the big apartment and its four windows, and uses the small one when he visits Paris.

In the early 18th century and through to the 19th, when the apartment was briefly home to the future emperor of France, Napoleon III, these first-floor rooms were formal reception rooms, lavishly decorated and furnished. Architect Paul Collier has managed to slot all the requirements of 21st-century life into a single window bay of a once stupendous room while retaining much of its past nobility.

The immensely high ceiling allows space for a generously proportioned mezzanine bedroom and bathroom hovering somewhere about halfway up the original chimney breast. The 21st-century architectural additions, such as the plain oak staircase, the high-tech kitchen, and the tubular metal rails at the top of the stairs and across the balcony, are explicitly modern, but their simple elegance fits well with the restrained classical detail of the plaster mouldings. From the bed there is a magnificent view over the Place Vendôme. Voile curtains can be pulled across for privacy. The bathroom, with its grand Deco-style fittings, is above the small entrance lobby to the apartment and is fully enclosed.

Over the years the interior had been changed so often that the only remaining original feature was the window itself and a heavy ceiling cornice. The cornice was restored and, with permission, the window was replaced with an exact copy using a 19th-century bronze replica of an 18th-century *espagnolette*, a traditional French window fastening. Paul Collier also installed a herringbone parquet floor using old oak boards and added applied mouldings below the cornice and on the chimney breast in a subdued version of 18th-century classical style.

The towering ceiling allowed him to insert a mezzanine floor above the dining area to house a bedroom and an open-plan bathroom. A compact Bulthaup kitchen including a sink, hob and fridge is housed in an opaque white glass column beneath the mezzanine and a neat oak staircase winds up behind it, while the boiler, washing machine and tumble drier are hidden in cupboards under the stairs. The minimal modernity of the kitchen, new staircase and mezzanine handrail makes it clear that these are contemporary inserts in a classical shell, but the restrained elegance of both styles is pleasingly complementary.

FAR LEFT Although the architectural bones of this room are old-fashioned, with its ornate cornice, high skirtings/baseboards and carved marble fireplace, the furnishings are contemporary. Formality is established in the symmetry of glass candlesticks and little vases on the mantelpiece and the pair of stools, which offer extra seating on the hearth, but equally subverted by the placing of a stool opposite the sofa and the outsize standard lamp to the left of the chimney breast.

LEFT and BELOW The floor-to-ceiling windows in the raised ground-floor drawing room had been partially blocked in. Opening them up to their original design sweeping down almost to floor level restored the lofty proportions of the room and allowed light to flood in. The square opening between the drawing room and dining room, BELOW, means that these rooms are lit from the front and the back of the house. A decorative theme of animals and plants links the separate spaces, with a leaf-patterned rug, a faux bois mirror, and the wall-mounted cases of butterflies and birds. These pick up on the details of the cornice and fireplace as well as making witty reference to the 19th-century fashion for collections and taxidermy.

# living in the middle

*To occupy a whole house in the centre of a city like London or New York is a privilege, but a privilege that generally comes with two disadvantages. Because inner-city land is so valuable, houses are almost always taller than they are wide, and a garden bigger than a couple of parking spaces is a rarity.*

Gael Towey, who is Creative Director for Martha Stewart Omnimedia, and her husband Stephen Doyle, a graphic designer, have nearly side-stepped the first disadvantage and are fortunate enough to live in a house that retains its park-like communal garden.

Their Italianate and Greek-style brownstone townhouse in Greenwich Village was built in the 1850s on four floors. The basement would originally have been the preserve of servants, the raised ground floor contained the reception rooms and the two upper floors bedrooms. Gael, Stephen and their two teenage children occupy the house very differently. Although they have

The house had been divided into two separate flats and the first floor was the living room and kitchen of the upper flat. Instead of reconverting it to bedrooms, the Toweys kept it as an open-plan family sitting room and kitchen. Black-and-white photographs propped on plain shelving make an attractive, moveable display.

*ABOVE* The formal dining room on the floor below has a wall of storage for books and files, and neatly incorporates desk space. The sleek, modern design of the cabinets renders them stylishly unobtrusive in their period setting.

retained the grand reception rooms, and have a small galley kitchen in the basement, their main living space is on the first floor, which opens onto a sizeable roof terrace over a later back extension. Their three bedrooms and two bathrooms are on the floor above. Instead of having to trek up three flights of stairs from the kitchen to the bedrooms – a journey that seems necessary many times a day for even the most organized – they spend most of their time living on two floors.

Although this arrangement appears to have been worked out for maximum convenience, in fact it is a legacy of how they first occupied the building. 'It does work brilliantly as a family home,' says Gael, 'but it wasn't exactly planned.' For ten years the family lived on the top two floors of the house while an old lady occupied the ground floor and basement. 'We had a bedroom, living room and kitchen on the first floor,' Gael explains, 'and the children had the whole top

floor as one big open space, with a tyre swing and enough space for them to ride their bikes round.'

When the lower two floors became available, the couple bought them and began to put the house back into one. Fortunately, despite having been divided, the reception rooms were intact, complete with original marble chimney pieces and ornate plaster cornicing. The lower half of the staircase had also survived and they copied its design to continue the stairs to the top floors.

The enfilade of three grand reception rooms now comprises their drawing room, which leads into a dining room and library combined, and through to a study at the back of the house. High ceilings, pairs of tall windows at either end, and the centrally placed fireplaces give these rooms a certain formality, which is reflected in the symmetry of the furnishings. This is the entertaining floor and the 'quiet floor', a place to gather with guests or to retreat to read or study.

They could have moved their main kitchen down to the lower ground floor but they decided they would miss eating outside on the roof terrace

*FAR LEFT* The first floor, which would once have been divided into bedrooms, is now a completely open-plan space with an oblong box inserted into the middle. This internal 'room' works hard for its size, acting as a divider between the kitchen, dining and living areas, and containing a cloakroom and utility room, a built-in music system and storage at one end, and a fridge at the kitchen end.

*ABOVE LEFT* Looking back from the kitchen area, past the fridge, there is a view of the main staircase. The original 19th-century staircase had survived to first-floor level and was copied to continue on to the top-floor bedrooms.

*BELOW LEFT* The left-hand side of the central 'room', looking towards the kitchen, is the informal dining area, decoratively linked to the living end of the room by the continuation of the shelving where rows of pictures are propped. The Murano glass chandelier centred above the table helps to give the space a character of its own and ensure it doesn't feel like a corridor.

*ABOVE* New glass windows and French doors open onto a large roof terrace at first-floor level above a later extension at the back of the house. From here the views are surprisingly verdant, across the magnolias and hydrangeas of the communal gardens.

overlooking the gardens. Instead they used the space for guest bedrooms, and an informal living room with an entertainment system and a galley kitchen — a place for the children to escape to when other rooms are in use for entertaining.

Although the façade of the house is protected, and even the exterior paint colour must be approved, internally they were free to move walls to suit. The first floor is one big open space with the bright white kitchen at one end and seating at the other. In the middle they have cleverly inserted a long, thin, windowless room, which works extremely hard considering how little space it occupies, housing the air-conditioning, a cloakroom in the middle, the refrigerator, and a stereo and storage at the living-room end.

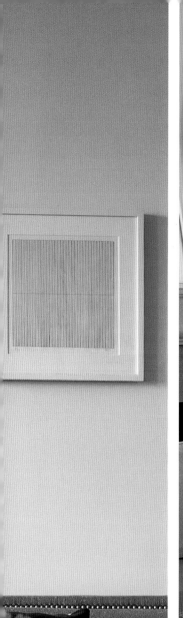

# classic single

LEFT and ABOVE A well-proportioned reception room with high ceilings makes this compact, one-bedroom, purpose-built apartment seem bigger than its actual square footage. Carefully chosen furnishings, such as the glass coffee table and the slim-legged chairs, sofa and dining table, help to magnify the floor space. Timothy Whealon added the panel mouldings to give the room a hint of classical grandeur.

'These apartments were made for bachelors and bachelorettes and, being a bachelor myself, this one suits me perfectly,' says interior designer Timothy Whealon. It seems that the needs of the single urbanite have changed little since 1922. The block was designed by renowned American architect Emery Roth and built by the improbably named firm of Bing & Bing in the heart of Greenwich Village. Each apartment has a generous living room, a bedroom, a bathroom and a tiny kitchen. Presumably then, as now, single urbanites dined out more often than in.

However, despite being a compact nine hundred square feet (ninety square metres), there are plenty of fitted cupboards and the ceilings are ten feet (three metres) high. When Timothy Whealon bought the apartment it had been modernized with a new marble bathroom and white Formica kitchen units. The arrangement of rooms, however, had not been tampered with because, as Whealon says, 'the original layout was perfect'. He should have said almost perfect. He made two structural changes to improve on its perfection, raising the height of the doors to match the height of the windows, and adding a pair of double doors linking the bedroom to the living room. 'Raising the doors,' he explains, 'helps the proportions, and the new double doors when left open expand the space in the bedroom and the living room by giving a view through from one to the other.'

The living room is in restrained classical style with a row of three sash windows, a central fireplace and elegant wall mouldings. Timothy Whealon restored and replaced the wall mouldings and exchanged the wooden chimney piece for a simple, bolection limestone surround, which he felt was more in keeping with the formal qualities of the room. 'I tried to keep to the spirit of the 1922 architecture but bring it a little bit up to date.'

Where later additions ran counter to this spirit he removed them. Ugly radiator covers were pulled out and replaced by ones that match the original mouldings. The bathroom was restored to its pre-war glory, copied from bathrooms in the same block that had never been changed. Tiling is in cream 'subway' bricks, the taps are nickel-plated and there is a fixed showerhead over the bath the size

The apartments were designed for single people at a time when the middle classes rarely cooked for themselves at home. The kitchen is only just over nine by seven feet (three by two metres) square. Timothy Whealon has made the most of this limited space by installing fitted cupboards that stretch up to the ceiling. The floor is the original cement, scored into squares and polished to look like stone paving. A fitted wooden banquette provides comfortable seating with storage beneath, next to a tiny table just big enough for a modest breakfast for one.

*LEFT* The exquisitely sophisticated colour scheme of palest greys, off-whites and honey-browns, with studied accents of charcoal and black, ties the rooms together. Furnishings are a confident mix of contemporary and antique, including unusual and eye-catching pieces such as the 1940s shell-shaped plaster wall sconces. The traditional shape of the sofa is given a contemporary edge by the choice of a rough linen sacking upholstery, smartly finished at the edges with rows of close nailing.

of a dinner plate. Early 20th-century American plumbing was sophisticated and luxurious even by modern standards, so this old-fashioned bathroom is as practical as it is handsome.

In the diminutive kitchen Whealon took out the Formica, which looked 'too new', and put in white-painted wooden cabinets. The old cement floor was intact under later tiling and he was able to restore and polish it. Despite the stainless-steel oven and extractor fan, this room, like the bathroom, has a vintage feel.

Timothy Whealon has worked hard to respect and enhance the architectural legacy of Emery Roth. He has been careful to retain and restore all the features of the apartment that have survived the decorating enthusiasms and fashions of subsequent decades, and his own alterations and additions are in keeping. But the result is far from a museum piece. Thanks to the way the rooms are decorated and furnished, the apartment is fresh and contemporary

'I wanted the spaces to flow into one another,' he says, 'and I wanted to make it as light and airy as possible.' Walls and woodwork are painted throughout in shades of palest grey and cream. Light reflects from the old red oak flooring, which has been bleached, washed with paint and polished to a shine. Decorative links between the separate rooms include the use of fabrics such as an eau-de-Nil linen, which appears as cushions in the living room and the bedroom and as a shower curtain in the bathroom. Furnishings are a stylish assembly of 'pieces I love', and juxtapose 18th-century elegance with quirky 20th century finds such as the 1940s plaster wall sconces. Emery Roth would surely approve.

*LEFT and ABOVE* One advantage of living alone is not having to close doors, and when the doors between rooms are left open the apartment feels more like an open-plan space. Timothy Whealon enhanced the sense of spatial flow by raising the door heights and by adding double doors that link the bedroom with the living room, allowing a view from the desk in the window of the bedroom through to the fireplace and vice versa.

*RIGHT* The original designers of these apartments sensibly allowed plenty of space for fitted cupboards. There are two large closets in the entrance hall, freeing up space in the bedroom for a capacious armchair and a desk so that it almost feels like an extension of the living room. The fitted cupboard in the living room has been converted into a bar, in effect adding a small extension to the kitchen.

The rooms' sizes, and some of the architectural details such as the plain, chunky cornices and high skirtings/ baseboards of this Edwardian flat, owe something to the Queen Anne Revival style popular at the beginning of the last century, and make an appropriate setting for the recent addition of an early Georgian marble chimney piece.

# getting things in proportion

*As an antique dealer and co-owner of Jamb Ltd, Will Fisher was well placed to furnish his Edwardian flat. But when he took possession, having bought at auction on the strength of a cursory viewing, he realized the flat needed more than furniture. On the third floor of a purpose-built block in North London, its layout had been 'messed around with'. Cornicing disappeared where partition walls had been added and the entrance hall had been split into a smaller lobby and a windowless space 'like a World War II bunker'.*

'There is nothing uglier,' Will continues, 'than a space that has been chopped and changed. The first thing I wanted to do was to make it feel integral again. I didn't necessarily put it back to how it was originally – but I opened up the hall, and nicked a bit of space from the bathroom to make the kitchen bigger.' He also blocked up the door which led into the kitchen from the hall and installed a magnificent pair of mid-19th-century double doors, which he 'happened to have lying around', to link living room and kitchen instead.

The doors were not the only architectural addition. One of Will's passions is what he calls 'the early English fireplace'. Two beautiful examples dating from the beginning of the 18th century have found a place in the flat, one in the living room and one in the bedroom. Both replace original chimney pieces, which had been removed and boarded over. In the bathroom he panelled the walls floor to ceiling in painted MDF, and tall fitted cupboards in the bedroom are made with Victorian panelled doors. Even the flooring is new to the flat – bleached pine boards that were once shelving in a cheese factory.

Like all the best antique dealers Will Fisher is a consummate recycler. So it is no surprise to learn that the kitchen work surfaces

*FAR LEFT* Adding to the well-worn, period feel of the living room are the wide floorboards, typical of Georgian interiors. In fact they are new to the flat and started life as shelving in an old cheese factory. A magnificent mahogany, glass-fronted bookcase, designed for the British Museum in the early 19th century by Sir Robert Smirke, towers behind the sleek lines of a buttoned leather Knoll sofa, which is at least a hundred and fifty years its junior. Despite the age gap, the pieces share a masculine elegance which renders them entirely compatible.

*LEFT and INSERT* Will Fisher added an opening to fit a pair of glossy mahogany doors dating from the 1850s, which now link the living room and kitchen. At the same time he blocked in the door that led from the hall into the kitchen. The opening perfectly frames the stainless-steel Smeg oven, but the feel of the kitchen is quite old-fashioned thanks to the brick-shaped wall tiles, the reclaimed teak work surfaces and the row of four pendant glass lamps, which match the date of the flat itself. The skull on the marble-topped table in the living room is that of a hippopotamus.

*ABOVE and BELOW RIGHT* Having pinched some space from the bathroom to make the kitchen bigger, Will Fisher restored its dignity by lining the walls with fielded panelling in painted MDF. The fittings are all period in style, including the high-level cistern and the roll-top bath, and the chrome-framed Art Deco mirror was salvaged from a demolished City bank.

*INSERT* A pair of wall-mounted vintage lights looms over an 18th-century chest of drawers in the bedroom. The cast-iron fin radiator is a reconditioned antique.

The meeting of styles and periods continues in this room, with a contemporary painting by Andrew Wallace hanging above another early English chimney piece. The modern bed has a stainless-steel base with wheels that have brakes 'like a hospital trolley'. The battered library chair in red Morocco leather dates from 1890; the bedside chest is also 19th century.

are reclaimed teak, that the hanging utensil rack was made from two butcher's shop fittings welded together and that the aluminium wall cupboards, which look terribly modish, are genuine 1950s.

What is a surprise is how well these disparate elements and periods work together. Will Fisher thinks this is partly because, once adjusted, the basic proportions of the rooms were good, and partly because he has chosen architectural elements and materials that already have a patina of use. In the living room, for example, the ten-foot (three-metre) ceilings, the high skirting boards/baseboards and the unusually wide floorboards make an appropriate setting for the early Georgian fireplace. The glossy mahogany doors add a flourish of grandeur.

The kitchen and the bathroom have a more Edwardian feel, perfectly in tune with the date of the flat. In the kitchen this is established by the brick-shaped cream tiles that line the walls and the row of four antique glass pendant lamps. As well as giving the kitchen a period feel, despite its contemporary centrepiece of a brushed stainless-steel oven, the way the bricks stop short of the ceiling lowers the height in this relatively small space and improves its proportions.

Fielded panelling in the bathroom is the equivalent of the cream bricks in the kitchen. The bath, basin and toilet are all old-fashioned designs, while being entirely practical, although the wall-mounted shower is still awaiting a shower curtain and is yet to be used.

Furnishings are a mix of favourite pieces including a magnificent glass-fronted bookcase from the British Museum and a ladder from the same source to reach its upper shelves. Again periods and styles are mixed, coming right up to date with the leather and chrome Knoll sofa and contemporary paintings on the walls.

'My aim was to create an interior that looked as though it had been undisturbed for some time. Now the flat is finished, with not a disappearing cornice in sight, Will Fisher has done just that.

*ABOVE* With the help of landscape gardener Sean Walters of The Plant Specialist, Neisha has made the most of the sheltered location of her mews house. Mirrored candle sconces gleam on the ivy-clad wall of her dining terrace, where the round table is by a friend, Rachel Schwalm, and the chairs are by Ron Arad from the Conran Shop.

*LEFT* Leaves entwined in a wire support frame the doorway into Neisha's kitchen, once the office cloakroom of the business that previously occupied the site. Because the site is securely enclosed, doors can be left open on warm days, a rare urban privilege.

*ABOVE RIGHT* The doors to the left of the dining terrace lead into the open-plan dining and living room. Evergreen planting means that, even in winter, the space is green and leafy. On a summer evening, when the candles are lighted, the space feels like an airy room, its ceiling open to the stars.

# urban oasis

*In the 19th century London was a city of horses. There were thousands of omnibuses on the roads, each using ten horses a day. There were also dustcarts, water carts, hansom cabs and carriages, all pulled by horses. To accommodate them, rows of stables were built with rooms above for the coachmen. They were called mews, which was the name of the cage used for hawks, because the royal stables, built in the 17th century, occupied the site where the King's hawks were once kept. The buildings continued to be referred to as the Royal Mews and the name was adopted to refer to all urban stabling.*

Ever since the combustion engine took over from horsepower, mews buildings have been steadily converted into garages and houses. Although small, their location, tucked away behind busy streets, makes them attractive places to live.

Pattern and textile designer and Chelsea retailer Neisha Crosland describes the South London mews where she lives with her husband and two young sons as like 'a little oasis'. The original stables, on either side of a long cobbled yard, had been converted into eight houses, but in the Second World War the mews was bombed, leaving only one of these standing by the gated entrance from the road. After the war another house was built opposite it on the other

*RIGHT* The small kitchen leads off the dining end of the living room and has a serving hatch above the oven so that dishes can be handed straight to the table. A door opens onto the courtyard and the window above the sink is veiled in leaves. Small mirror tiles frame the view.

side of the gate, but the remainder of the plot was used as garaging and commercial storage. Neisha bought first one house, then the other, and linked the two with a single room, which bridges the cobbles at first-floor level. The ground floor of the house on the right is rented out but its first floor provides invaluable extra space, including a playroom and utility room.

Although both houses had been occupied by families after the war, more recently the site was used as offices. Neisha and her French husband Stephan hired Marius Barran as their architect and set about turning the buildings back into a home. There were few original architectural features, just a small bedroom fireplace where perhaps a coachman once warmed his hands, but the whole plot had a sense of history, which they have been careful to preserve. In the

*ABOVE* **The living room with its dining table at one end is as colourful and fresh as a fruit salad, although Neisha describes the difference between the green of the walls and the darker green of the woodwork more prosaically as 'frozen peas' and 'tinned peas'.**

*RIGHT* **The George Smith sofa upholstered in strawberry red is scattered with Neisha Crosland cushions, while more of her designs, mixed in with pictures by friends, hang in informal groupings on the wall above.**

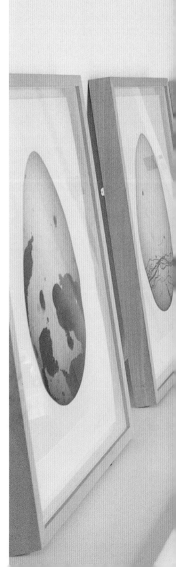

fireplace they installed in the downstairs living room they used a slab of stone, found in the courtyard, as a mantelshelf, and a metal drainage grille, also found outside, as a fireback.

Outside they have kept the cobbles and transformed the concreted-over gap where the remaining stables once stood into lawn. Thanks to the old brick walls, which still surround the plot, it makes a delightfully sheltered and secluded garden. With the help of garden designer Sean Walters, Neisha planted evergreens, including holly, jasmine and ivy, so the garden is green all year round. 'You can literally smell the chlorophyll as you come through the gates off the street,' she says.

The entire ground floor of the left-hand house is a living and dining room with a kitchen opening off it. A wall of French doors opens onto a terrace where a table and chairs invite alfresco dining. Upstairs are two bedrooms and a bathroom, an attic bedroom, and the bridging room, which is used as a home office and gym.

This last room is white but the rest of the house is bright with colour: greens, reds, yellows and blues in exuberant and unexpected combinations. Furniture is mostly antique, but contemporary works of art and unusual lighting, both new and vintage, give the house a decidedly quirky feel. Neisha is as unafraid of colour as she is of putting furnishings together in eccentric juxtapositions. Above the living-room mantelpiece, instead of the prized picture or mirror you might expect, there is a large plasma-screen television. It shouldn't work but, like the colours, it looks surprisingly good.

*ABOVE LEFT*  The upstairs rooms were once occupied by grooms who lived above the stables, but there was little left in the way of period features. Instead Neisha has added her own character, filling every space including this, her bathroom, with colour and visual interest.

*ABOVE RIGHT*  The main bedroom still has a small fireplace, a lone architectural survival from the building's past. The quilt is a 'very old favourite', the cushions are from Judy Greenwood, and the curtains are Neisha's own creation, made from Indian scarves.

*RIGHT*  Linking the two separate houses that stand on either side of the entrance gateway is a completely new room, which forms a bridge at first-floor level. As a contrast to the rest of the house, the walls are pristine white and the floor is painted in a pale chequerboard.

# urban chic furniture and lighting

The decorator Syrie Maugham might be considered the patron saint of urban chic. Her seminal 'all white' drawing room, designed in the 1930s, still looks chic and contemporary today, with its white walls and ceiling, its long, low sofa and boxy armchairs upholstered in beige, and its huge rug in two tones of cream, all reflected and refracted in a tall screen of mirror glass standing behind the sofa.

The essentials of this style have been endlessly imitated: the pale, plain upholstery; the palette of whites, off-whites and nearly white honey-brown; the horizontal emphasis of the furnishings; all have become the stock-in-trade of the sharp, urban interior. Not only are the shades of white and neutral soothing to the eye, they seem to suggest a life of pristine elegance, unencumbered by children with sticky hands or dogs with muddy feet.

There is a family-friendly version of urban chic, as exemplified by the homes of Gael Towey and Neisha Crosland. In these houses there is colour and even the beginnings of clutter. What makes them sophisticated is the way they mix the former and arrange the latter, with wit and with an artist's eye.

**SOFT FURNISHINGS** should be long, low, and clean-lined like Syrie Maugham's. This is the territory of the fashionable L-shaped sofa, a sociable and space-efficient form of seating.

**FITTED FURNITURE**, whether bedroom wardrobes or drawing-room bookshelves, not only maximizes storage, it also helps to keep the contents of a room streamlined.

**IT IS MUCH EASIER** to create a sophisticated look if you stick to a very limited colour palette. Pale colours in neutral shades always look expensively high-maintenance.

**A STRICT COLOUR PALETTE** also helps to bind together different styles and periods of furnishing. Frédéric Méchiche is a master of this, putting iconic pieces of 20th-century furniture next to classical French antiques, united by the house colour scheme of black, white and cream.

**IF YOU ARE GUTTING** a house, it might be worth considering having built-in speakers or even a sound system with speakers in every room.

THE OCCASIONAL ANTIQUE in a room furnished with contemporary furniture or a couple of sleek modern pieces in a room furnished with antiques makes both the old and the new look more intriguing.

A FIREPLACE is a far more attractive focus for a room than a television, and no longer need it be traditional. There is now a wide choice of very modern fireplaces, often designed for gas-effect fires and ranging in style from the wacky to the ultra cool.

STEREOS AND TELEVISIONS can come out of their cupboards. Some of today's designs are so smart they can be wall-mounted like a piece of art. Neisha Crosland has her flat-screen television above her mantelpiece, making them a joint focus of the room.

LIGHTING can be as flexible and clever as you can afford, with schemes devised specially for each room and a series of different settings to create different moods at the touch of a switch. Even on a budget you can create a range of effects with judiciously placed table and standard lamps, each on a separate switch.

THERE OFTEN seems to be a better choice of good-quality, affordable and stylish contemporary lighting than furniture. A few well-chosen modern lights can lift a room of otherwise traditional furnishings from the mundane to the exciting.

# urban chic fabric and finishing touches

Urban chic favours plain walls, plain floors, whether wood, stone or an expanse of uninterrupted neutral carpet, and plain fabrics. This makes for a demanding interior — we all know why hotels favour patterned carpets and upholstery. The ubiquitous cream sofa, which at one stage was almost the *sine qua non* of the urban chic interior, shows every scuff, attracting dirt almost as quickly as fluffy white towels acquire grey smudges.

As well as being potentially impractical, plain fabrics can be as difficult to mix together as patterns. Big blocks of a single colour need balancing, one with the other, and texture becomes more important the less visual distraction there is.

Plain backgrounds, however, make an ideal setting for paintings and decorative objects. A plain sofa frames a richly figured cushion like the mount for a picture, and pictures themselves can hang on a plain wall without having to fight for attention. Accessorizing a room of simple, elegant furniture and adding splashes of pattern, a coloured glass vase with a striking silhouette, a small piece of modern sculpture, or a big vase of blowsy peonies, is an art and a pleasure. This is the fun after the hard work of getting the basics right.

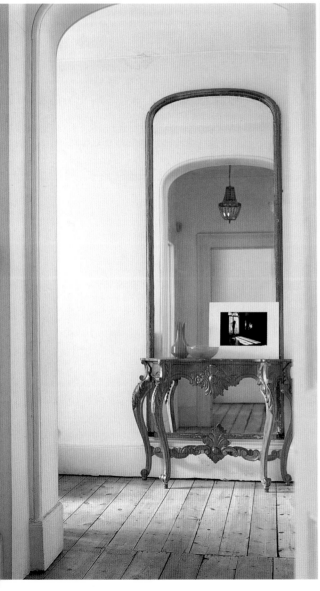

A SLIGHTLY MORE PRACTICAL ALTERNATIVE to cream upholstery is the pale taupe of unbleached linen. If it has to be cream or off-white, have washable loose covers, ideally shrink-proof ones that can be thrown in the washing machine.

OLD LINEN AND HEMP SHEETS are surprisingly sturdy and, depending on their weight, make beautiful upholstery or curtains. The texture can vary from rough and heavy to fine and smooth. Hemp is always coarser.

THE PLAINER THE FABRIC, the more noticeable its texture. Use tactile velvet and corduroy for upholstery, and cashmere, mohair, satin and tweed for strokeable cushions.

LEATHER AND SUEDE are at their best in a plain colour and come with the added bonus of their deliciously expensive smell, and a texture and 'handle' that is irresistible. The real thing is worth the price because, unlike a synthetic imitation, it will actually improve with age.

FUR looks as glamorous in a room as on an old-fashioned movie star. Save your conscience by choosing fake fur for throws, and sheepskins or cowskins for rugs — the bigger, the smarter.

BIG, BOLD STRIPES in two colours are a way to introduce graphic pattern into a room full of plains/solids. Or you can add a stripe to a curtain or blind by lining its edges with a plain fabric in a contrasting colour.

LARGE PAINTINGS look more dramatic and stylish than groupings of small ones. If you only have small pictures, save them for small rooms.

BLACK-AND-WHITE PHOTOGRAPHS can be propped on a narrow shelf for a chic, moveable display. Put them in matching frames for a disciplined, uniform effect, or mix them up for a more bohemian, eclectic feel.

FRAME A PIECE OF A FAVOURITE FABRIC in a bold design as an inexpensive artwork that can be as big as you like. Choose a large-scale figurative repeat for maximum effect.

MIRROR adds space, light and gloss to an interior. Look for mirrored furniture as well as wall-mounted mirrors. Use mirror glass, cut to size, to transform an ordinary coffee, bedside, or occasional table into something altogether more desirable.

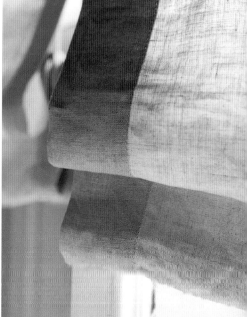

# RUSTIC

Three out of four of the houses in this chapter are in the country, but one is in London, albeit a leafy suburb. Rustic style is as much a function of architecture as location. A building begins to look rustic when its bare bones and raw fabric are revealed, whether the stone that forms the lintel of a door or the oak beams that support a roof. Natural materials, unadorned and on show, are the stylistic link between all these interiors, from the Norman arches of Hemingford Grey to the soaring timbers of a Surrey barn.

# oak-framed elegance

*LEFT and ABOVE* **This is an interior that seems to offer the best of all worlds: it has a genuinely rural feel and yet is close to the centre of a city, plus it has the light and open space of a modern building but also the character, sense of history, and architectural features of an old one. The combination makes a perfect setting for the beautifully made, simple, contemporary furniture that is the speciality of its owner.**

*If you were to find yourself magically transported into Michael D'Souza's living room without any clues about your new location, you might be tricked into thinking you were somewhere deeply rural. Six tall sash windows look out onto trees and a river beyond, and the ceiling is heavily oak beamed. An open ladder staircase leads to a top floor built into the massive gable of a roof with the structure of a timber-framed barn. It is a beautiful but puzzling interior, part industrial, part domestic and obviously very old.*

The river is the Thames and the address is a London suburb. Michael D'Souza lives in the top two floors of the only surviving building of The Mortlake Tapestry Works. Established in 1619 under the patronage of James I, this was once a hive of creativity, producing some of the finest and most famous tapestries of the 17th century, woven by up to a hundred and forty Dutch Lutheran craftsmen who had been headhunted and lured to England for their unique skill.

Once there were several buildings including a chapel. Now only the Upper Dutch House remains, where there was a workroom with looms and a studio for the master painter and designer plus apartments for bachelor weavers. Despite the fame and quality of the tapestries the business was never a financial success and the weavers often came close to starvation while they waited to be paid. In 1703 the works was closed.

Michael D'Souza cannot be sure whether his long, bright living room was designed as an art and design studio or for weaving. It is certainly well lit enough from its six windows to have been either. There are three further windows, which were blocked up in the 18th century to reduce window tax. Whatever its former use, today this building offers those two most desirable qualities – open space and lashings of daylight – with the added charm of old sash windows complete with shutters, wall panelling, wooden floors, and the sturdy grace of the structural oak beams.

In order to retain the rhythmic march of the six windows, Michael partitioned off space for an entrance hall, utility room, cloakroom and kitchen along the back wall. With an open staircase making a natural divide, the remaining space is separated into a living room at one end and a dining room at the other. Upstairs was unpartitioned when he bought it and he has divided it into two bedrooms at either end, and a bathroom in between alongside a landing so capacious that there is space for a study area and a music area with a piano.

While the beams give the interior a distinctly rustic flavour, the tall sash windows have a more urban elegance. Michael's decision to paint all

*ABOVE* A free-standing bath takes advantage of the extra height allowed by a dormer window. Standing in the bath for a shower you can see the river beyond the trees.

*LEFT* The unpainted timber that forms the architectural bones of the building finds a reflection in the natural wood of so many of its furnishings, like this safari-style chair with its leather seat and arms in a corner of a bedroom. The windows, tucked between beams, would be swamped by curtains. Instead plain Roman blinds leave the view of trees unimpeded.

*RIGHT* The practical disadvantages of a bedroom under the eaves are fully compensated for by the beauty of the framework of oak beams, perfectly engineered to support the roof.

the walls and the floorboards white in the main living area but only to wash down the oak beams, leaving them dark and slightly rough, serves to emphasize this contrast. The mix makes for a particularly sophisticated version of rustic style and is a perfect setting for modern furnishings from Michael D'Souza's Fulham shop Mufti, which specializes in clean-lined contemporary craftsmanship. Simple, modern tables and chairs in polished wood, a boxy armchair upholstered in linen, an ottoman sofa in suede – all combine a modern simplicity with traditional and natural materials and fit beautifully into this airy space.

Contrasts make for visual excitement. Here there is architectural contrast, between the beams and the windows, between the painted wall panelling and the ladder stairs, and also between the modernity of the furnishings and the age of the building. But there are also many visual, and even tactile, links. The colour palette is limited to white and shades of neutral and the choice of materials is similarly disciplined; the age-darkened oak of the beams is echoed in dark wood furnishings and accessories, and suede, leather, linen and animal skins all reoccur throughout the apartment.

*RIGHT* Sophisticated urban style meets the almost monastic simplicity of 17th-century French village architecture in the ground-floor living room. Now furnished with sleek sofas and a coffee table by Philippe Hurel, it is hard to imagine that this space would once have housed the family's livestock. The iron curtain rails were made by a local blacksmith.

*LEFT and BELOW* Bare stonework gives the house a raw, rustic elegance. There are two stone staircases, one leading straight up from the living room and rather quaintly housing a fireplace, the other rising up from the entrance hall to the left of the front door. At the foot of this staircase an ancient stone basin from a church is set into the deep window sill.

# stone aged

*Very occasionally you find a house that is already so perfect, you can simply move in and enjoy it. When an American art dealer took possession of La Louve, her house in Provence, she says it was more like inheriting a work of art than buying a home.*

Set on the edge of a village with views over farmland, the house dates back to the 17th century, a time when living quarters would have been on the first floor and the family's animals stabled below. Its deep walls are local stone, pale as porridge, partially rendered with lime plaster, and its roof is clad in gently undulating terracotta tiles. The interior has a simple, almost monastic quality, while the terraced garden beyond, a green and grey patchwork of stone and neatly clipped topiary, is a leafy sculpture park.

The house had already been restored and the garden created by the previous owner, French fashion and fabric designer Nicole de Vesian. The current owner loved it the moment she saw it and was determined that any changes she made would be in the spirit of Nicole's vision. Nicole had both enhanced the existing original features of the house and imported some of her own. In places she had stripped the walls back to the rough, random stone and exposed

*LEFT* The entrance hall was once a passage through which animals were led from the village into the fields. Its arched vaulting gives the interior an ancient and distinctly ecclesiastical feel, enhanced by the bench, which is a church pew. A layer of river pebbles covers the floor. Although not entirely practical, it makes an evocative link between garden and house.

*RIGHT* The 'summer kitchen' is a new alternative to the small 'winter kitchen', *BELOW*. Here again the stone arches, which once supported a road, have been left unplastered.

the honey-coloured wood of beams above doors. In one hallway between rooms she made a niche for an oval stone basin and put in a window above, reflecting its shape. In the entrance hall she set a church font into the wall.

Stone recurs throughout the house in the arched vaulting of the entrance hall, which was probably once a passageway for animals from the street to the fields; in the austere stone staircases which lead upstairs, one from the hall and one from the living room; as single-slab door thresholds; as shelving and simply as decoration, whether an arrangement of smooth pebbles or the rugged boulder which crouches under the shelf in a bedroom. The floor of the entrance hall is scattered with a deep layer of river pebbles. At first the new inhabitant thought this was taking the stony theme a step too far, but as she lived in the house she came to appreciate the way this indoor gravel linked the interior of the house with the paths and terraces outside.

Nicole de Vesian had not quite finished the house when she left it. The new owner called in François Gilles and Dominique Lubar of IPL

Interiors to help 'bring it into the 21st century and introduce a little more convenience, comfort and colour', as François puts it. An upstairs room at the back of the house was once the pigeon loft, with a row of small, square windows big enough for birds but too small to admit much natural light. This has now been converted into a spare bedroom with the addition of three extra

*ABOVE* When the internal walls were replastered, old-fashioned lime plaster was used and some stonework and structural beams were left uncovered, giving the house a primitive appeal. Lime plaster is appropriate for an old building because it breathes, unlike modern plaster, so can help to solve damp problems. The window bars were made by a local blacksmith, and add a new layer of traditional craftsmanship to the house. Another 'new' addition is this ancient font, *BELOW RIGHT*.

*RIGHT* The spare bedroom was once a pigeon loft, now made habitable by the addition of windows and a bath and basin, *BELOW FAR RIGHT*, cunningly hidden behind low walls. The walls provide a degree of separation without dividing the room in two.

*ABOVE FAR RIGHT* A rough wood shelf appears to be supported by a boulder. The contrast between rough-hewn stone and wood and the quilts on the bed makes the room cosy.

windows and an en suite bath and basin cunningly concealed behind low walls in the same natural stone as the walls of the room. The capacious bath and the mounded pillows on the bed seem all the more luxurious for their setting of roughly cut ceiling beams and exposed stonework.

A second additional room was created by converting a long, low outbuilding at right angles to the house into a 'summer kitchen'. Here again, there are deep vaulted arches, like in the entrance hall, and the cool, cave-like feel of the space makes it a perfect retreat on a hot summer day. The stone was left bare and

unplastered, just as Nicole would have left it, and wooden shelving has been installed in Nicole's favourite African hardwood.

As well as comfort, convenience and colour a fresh layer of modernity has been added to this profoundly rustic interior. There is appropriately chunky local pottery on the shelves of the new kitchen and the odd well-worn antique, but there is also an unashamedly contemporary Bulthaup kitchen in stainless steel. Like the lean, clean-lined sofas by Philippe Hurel in the living room, these slices of urban design make a sharp and pleasing contrast to their countrified setting.

# in the frame

*There is something irresistibly romantic about the idea of living in an old barn. Perhaps we are attracted by childhood images of the Nativity full of warm hay and the sweet breath of animals, or a desire to reconnect with an idealized rural life of the past when communities were small and people lived on what they grew. Aside from these pleasant associations, old timber-framed barns are feats of engineering with their skeleton of huge timbers, jointed, braced and cantilevered to make structures of strength and durability. Although they were not designed to be lived in, barns can offer the lofty, open spaces now so desirable as homes.*

*ABOVE* The kitchen occupies a smaller wooden-framed building at right angles to the main barn. Old bricks support the hob and work surfaces and fit well with the rustic, utilitarian feel of these spaces that were once the workplace of a farmer.

*LEFT and FAR LEFT* The main barn is thought to date from the mid-17th century and has a deep roof, which sinks lower to the ground on one side than the other. An extra room has been created in the midst of this huge, cathedral-like space by the addition of a mezzanine floor at one end. Reclaimed oak was used for its construction, carefully chosen to match the original timbers of the barn.

*ABOVE* The main barn sits on sloping land. The difference in height between the huge doors on either side, designed to be big enough for loaded carts to pass through, has been resolved with internal steps, one of which has been padded to make extra seating.

*ABOVE* Designed to house animals, or store grain, barns are never well endowed with windows. Here a row of new small, square apertures affords panoramic views from within without spoiling the appearance of the façade.

*LEFT* Some of the bedrooms have wall-to-wall natural matting, a material that seems particularly appropriate in rooms that feel almost medieval.

*RIGHT* In this bedroom, the beams that form the walls and support the roof find their match in the chunky bed base. The extreme simplicity of the bedroom furnishings could be too austere were it not for the sense of comfort and enclosure afforded by the surrounding woodwork.

Of course, you cannot simply move in and make yourself a bed of hay like Heidi. Old timber-framed barns do not have foundations, and usually have trodden mud floors. Built to house animals and store fodder, they may have huge doors to allow horse-drawn carts in and out, but they rarely have windows. Even when planning permission has been granted to convert a barn to domestic use, there may be restrictions on the size and number of new windows.

The new owners faced all these problems when they bought a group of farm buildings in the Surrey countryside. The main building was a fine barn, thought to date back to the mid-17th century. Adjoining it were further outbuildings forming three and a half sides of a square around a central courtyard, where an old photograph shows cows milling around before milking. They employed architect Joanna Jefferson to help put their ideas into practice.

The first task was to give the buildings a secure footing. All were stripped back to their wooden bones and jacked up onto a low supporting brick wall, which had been suitably

*ABOVE LEFT* **Despite its air of rough-hewn asceticism, this barn conversion incorporates all the luxuries of modern living, including three well-appointed bathrooms. Here, instead of timber, quarry tiles have been used for the flooring, another natural material in keeping with the rustic feel of the architecture.**

*BELOW LEFT* **When the four barns that make up this complex of farm buildings were divided into separate rooms, a lot of new joinery was required, for internal walls, windows, and doors. All the doors, like the one into this small cloakroom, were traditionally made, planked and braced, and fitted with old-fashioned wooden latches.**

*CENTRE* **The smaller barn that faces the kitchen across the courtyard was converted into two bedrooms and two bathrooms. This bathroom is separated from the room next to it by a wooden partition wall, which stops short of the ceiling so as not to interfere with the line of the roof timbers.**

*LEFT* **In a notable exception to the all-white, or all-white between wooden beams, rule that characterizes the rest of the house, this cloakroom's walls are lined with timber planking that has been painted in alternate stripes of white and dark blue. The effect is both smart and surprising.**

underpinned. With the buildings securely anchored, the spaces between the timbers were filled and insulated. Some inner walls are plaster, some are horizontal timber planks, and the outside of each building is wrapped in traditional black-stained timber cladding.

The owners were at great pains to preserve the 'dignity' of the buildings. The main barn with its magnificent roof, which sweeps down lower on one side than the other, was left as a single space. Because new windows were limited by planning restrictions, the two huge doors, which led through the barn, were partially glazed. One formed the front door with windows above, and the other is all glass and incorporates French doors opening onto the courtyard. To gain extra living space, a mezzanine floor was inserted into the roof space using reclaimed timbers carefully chosen to match the warm, battered oak of the original structure. The effect is seamless and the platform has the added advantage of creating a cosy, low-ceilinged area beneath, where sofas are gathered round a wood-burning stove.

Another design problem was posed by the difference in ground level between the doors on either side of the main barn. The elegant solution was a series of stone-capped brick steps leading down from the front door. Padded cushions convert the steps not used as a passageway into extra seating.

At a right angle to the main barn are a breakfast room and kitchen. The remaining outbuildings have been divided up to make four bedrooms and three bathrooms, also characterized by their enclosing framework of beams. In some rooms these have been painted white; in others, as in the main barn, they stand out in their natural shades of weathered brown from the white-painted walls between.

Floorings of matting, terracotta tiles, or oak boards, and simple wooden furnishings, are all perfectly in keeping with their rustic setting. Even the light switches are set into oak plates. The cows have long ago departed but the gentle, rural atmosphere remains undisturbed by the buildings' new inhabitants.

The first-floor room, which Lucy Boston renamed the music room in honour of her gramophone, was once the grand solar of the Norman household, with a carved fireplace and soaring ceiling. Today its exposed stonework and lime-washed walls make it seem more modest than magnificent.

*RIGHT* Lucy Boston uncovered the original Norman arched windows and added plain shutters. The old records entertained airmen during the war, when she held 'concerts' for them.

The manor house at Hemingford Grey near Huntingdon has been lived in continuously for more than eight hundred and fifty years. Its walls have sheltered Norman nobles, Tudor gentry, a family of famous Georgian beauties, Victorian farmers and, more recently, author and artist Lucy Boston, who immortalized it as 'Green Knowe' in a series of children's books. Today it is home to Diana Boston, Lucy's daughter-in-law.

# written
# in stone

*ABOVE and RIGHT* **When Lucy Boston bought the house, its Norman core had been divided to make several smaller rooms and a ceiling had been added to make attic bedrooms above the Norman solar. She partially removed this ceiling to restore the room to its former proportions. The gramophone dates from 1929.**

*OPPOSITE ABOVE* **An old cupboard is set into the hugely thick walls of the dining room. Lucy made the curtains from a Regency quilt, which inspired her to make her own patchworks. Many of them still adorn the house.**

*OPPOSITE BELOW* **The main bedroom is next to the music room and once formed part of the great Norman chamber. Over the centuries new layers of architecture were added to the house, including a Georgian façade giving this room a tall sash window.**

Despite its grand name, Hemingford Grey has only three bedrooms. But when it was first built in the mid-12th century it was a house of very high status. The surviving two-storey building was the private quarters of the lord of the manor, an upstairs solar with a fireplace and large windows, with storerooms beneath. There is no stone quarried locally, so every block and boulder of the four-feet (one-metre) thick walls was carted miles overland from Stamford. The adjoining great hall and fortifications have now gone.

Lucy Boston bought Hemingford Grey in 1937 and spent the next five years restoring it. Over the centuries the house had been repeatedly added to and altered. Lucy stripped away the various lean-tos that clustered around the original Norman core and removed internal partitions that had reduced the interior to a jumble of little rooms, one such an awkward shape it could only be entered on hands and knees.

On the ground floor she made a dining room. The floor above is now two rooms, the main bedroom and the music room. Over the bedroom is an attic, but Lucy took out the later ceiling in the music room so that the space soars into the roof vaults as it was designed to. The hall, kitchen, third bedroom and bathroom are in a Tudor extension.

As she unpicked the later layers of architecture Lucy found Norman windows and, in the music room, the remains of a great fireplace hidden behind cupboards. Elizabethan alterations had partly dismantled it to make way for a new window but miraculously the missing stones were still lying around in the garden. Lucy pieced it back together like a hefty jigsaw puzzle.

Furnishings are a collection of slightly battered antiques, patchworks made by Lucy Boston and simple block-printed fabrics by her friend Elisabeth Vellacott. There is still no central heating. Diana lights a fire in the Tudor fireplace in winter and keeps it going day and night to supplement her heaters. Aside from the cold, she says it is still a comfortable and lovely place to live.

# rustic furniture and lighting

Rustic style is a romantic idea, an escapist dream in a world of the mass-produced and the disposable. Running to keep up with technology, and materially sated, we cannot shake off an enduring nostalgia for a pre-industrial rural way of life when almost everything, from what we wore to what we sat on, was made locally and on a small scale. We know perfectly well that life for the average 18th-century farmer was tough. What we seek when we choose to live in a rustic building furnished with rustic charm is to recreate a flavour of that earthy reality without, of course, having to compromise on modern luxury and convenience.

In fact, rustic buildings with their exposed, roughly adzed beams, bare stonework, flagged or boarded floors, and lime-washed walls can make the perfect foil for sophisticated furnishings, as long as the sophistication is of the pared-down, clean-lined variety, as in Michael D'Souza's house. Natural materials are appropriate to the philosophy as well as the style. Whether old or new, sleek or a little bit scruffy, rustic furnishings should give the appearance of an artless simplicity, however clever and complex the plumbing and the sound system.

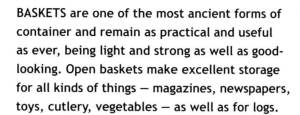

BASKETS are one of the most ancient forms of container and remain as practical and useful as ever, being light and strong as well as good-looking. Open baskets make excellent storage for all kinds of things — magazines, newspapers, toys, cutlery, vegetables — as well as for logs.

LINE A WICKER HAMPER with plain cotton — old sheets are ideal — to make it dustproof and use it to store clothes or towels.

WICKER ARMCHAIRS can be surprisingly comfortable, especially when well padded, and are easy to move around a room when you want to change seating arrangements, unlike their heavy, wooden-framed equivalents.

A RUSTIC INTERIOR is the ideal setting for an unfitted kitchen. Look for free-standing dressers and sideboards. Inexpensive new or second-hand pine furniture can be painted to hide its tell-tale orange grain.

OPEN SHELVES in a kitchen have a more country feel than wall cupboards. Use them for anything that is in constant use and gets washed or wiped regularly; otherwise they will collect unappetizing dust.

COFFEE TABLES were introduced into living rooms with the advent of television, so you will never find an antique example. However, an old pine chest or a canvas and leather trunk with a flat top makes a good alternative.

AN OLD PLANKED DOOR, as long as it is not badly warped, can make an attractive table-top, sanded and resting on trestles.

HAVE A GO at making your own furniture using salvaged wood, whether old ceiling joists or railway sleepers/ties. The converted barn in Surrey has a coffee table made from two giant beams mounted on casters and a bed with a similarly hefty frame in old wood, also on wheels.

BEAMS provide an ideal fixing point for discreet spotlights, whether a ceiling is flat or sloping.

LOOK FOR LAMPSHADES in natural materials like parchment, bark and even feather. Wickerwork lampshades cast particularly pretty shadows.

EXPLORE THE SKILLS of your local craftsmen. A blacksmith, for example, may be prepared to make all kinds of things to your own design, from fire-irons, to curtain poles, to bedsteads, to a hanging lantern. A basket-maker might be prepared to make something bespoke, and then, for a moment, you can pretend you are an 18th-century farmer.

# rustic fabric and finishing touches

Making a piece of fabric by hand and from scratch is an incredibly labour-intensive business, as anyone knows who has carded and spun woollen fleece or worked at a handloom. Before machinery took over, the fabrics that inched their way from weavers' looms were highly valued, however coarse. Imported silks, velvets and damasks were the privilege of a tiny minority who could afford them.

The most appropriate fabrics for a modern interpretation of a rustic interior are those that would have been produced by and for rural communities, such as linen, hemp, and wool. Cotton, first grown in India, only became widely available in the 19th century. Unlike other imports, it was relatively cheap and soon found its place at the windows and on the beds of even quite humble country houses. Because it took colour so well, it could be block- or roller-printed, bringing affordable pattern into people's homes for the first time.

The simple furniture and sturdy, practical fabrics that create a rustic feel do not invite anything elaborate in the way of pictures and ornaments. The rustic interior is far from minimal, but nor is it loaded down with knick-knacks. Stick to the famous maxim of William Morris and have only what 'you know to be useful, or believe to be beautiful' in your rustic home, and you won't go wrong.

**RECYCLE FABRICS** like they did in the days when everything was used and reused until it literally disintegrated. Make a patchwork from outgrown children's clothes or out-of-fashion summer dresses. Start with a cushion and you might even graduate to a pair of curtains like those at Hemingford Grey.

**ANTIQUE LINEN SHEETS** have already been mentioned for curtains and upholstery. Those from poorer households tend to be thick and rough, with a texture far more comfortable for furnishings than bed linen. Hemp was the poor man's linen and has a particularly attractive, nubbly texture and a heavy drape.

**SACKING** may seem like an unlikely candidate for interior use, but it makes surprisingly chic curtains.

STRIPED TICKINGS are available in a wide range of colours and make attractive curtains and cushions. Ginghams have a similarly innocent, country appeal. Both mix well with florals and toiles.

UNLINED CURTAINS look fresher and much less grand than anything lined and interlined. However, unless they are made in a thick heavy fabric, they will not be effective at blocking light or draughts.

CURTAINS gathered on curtain wire or slim metal rods make cheap and pretty cupboard doors. Hang them across the corner of a bedroom to make a small, triangular wardrobe, in front of kitchen shelves to keep out the dust, or as a skirt round washbasins to hide the spare toilet paper and bleach.

LANDSCAPES AND SEASCAPES are particularly at home on rough country walls, but not in fancy gilt frames. You might even find the work of a local artist that you admire.

POTTERY always looks more bucolic than fine china or porcelain. Again, see if you can source the work of someone local. You might even decide to commission a whole dinner service.

FOUND OBJECTS — nests, pebbles, driftwood and shells — can be as extraordinary and beautiful as any sculpture or work of art.

# RECYCLED SPACES

Recycled is a statement
of fact rather than
a description of a style.
Many houses in this book
had former, less domestic,
lives before reverting to
their original purposes
as homes: one was
a consumption clinic,
one a tripe merchant's,
another a sweatshop.
What distinguishes the
homes in this chapter
is that they have been
created in buildings that
were not designed to be
lived in. Some, like the
former dame school, have
taken to their new
existence with ease;
others, like the New York
loading bay, have had to
be persuaded, but all
retain a tantalizing flavour
of their past, which only
adds to their attraction.

*ABOVE* When Evan Snyderman moved in he took down the later partition walls and redivided the enormous floor space, once classrooms in the building that was Public School 52, to make three bedrooms, two studios and this vast living room. The iron columns are two of eight original structural supports. Furnishings include mid-20th-century 'finds', which Evan collected long before they were fashionable.

*RIGHT* The original flooring had not survived, except in the cloakroom area, where it was slate. Working to a tight budget, Snyderman put down sheets of plywood and painted it a smoky blue-grey with hard-wearing floor paint. This cheap solution is both practical and good-looking.

# back to the classroom

People are fond of describing their house before renovation as 'a wreck'. Usually it is a slight exaggeration employed to convey the misery of invasive plaster dust and the endless cups of tea required by resident builders. Evan Snyderman spent the first six months in his new home camping in the middle of the floor and sleeping in a tent, because it really was a wreck.

*LEFT* Some original architectural features survived, including the ornate pressed-tin ceiling at one end of the living space, and part of a glazed partition, which may have enclosed the principal's office. The more domestic nature of these 19th-century features makes an interesting contrast with the industrial feel of the stripped brick walls and the metal ducting, which carries wiring across the high ceilings.

*RIGHT* The area thought to have been the principal's office has a raised timber floor and is now an open-plan kitchen. There are no smart fitted cupboards, just a fridge, an oven, a sink and a home-made work surface and shelves. This room, like the rest of the apartment, was fitted out at minimal expense, but who needs fancy fittings with space and light on this scale?

'The windows were cemented over, there was a huge mound of rubble because the floor above had been gutted and the results chucked down through a hole in my ceiling, there was no plumbing, no electricity, and no heating. I really needed that tent and sleeping bag.'

Evan Snyderman moved in with a pile of rubble because it was inexpensive and he was looking for studio space for his work as a sculptor, and because he could see past the mess to the huge potential beyond. The building had been Public School 52, established in 1890, its claim to fame the fact that its principal was the first woman to be appointed to such a position.

It has a handsome three-storey red-brick façade, a bell tower, high ceilings inside and large windows. Old photographs show that it once stood in the middle of fields. When Evan arrived the hedges had long been torn up in favour of bricks, concrete and tarmac, and the area had declined. 'Back then in the early '90s I felt like a real pioneer,' he says. 'Twenty years on it's a trendy place to live.'

His lease was for the whole first floor, five thousand square feet (five hundred square metres) of it. The landlord had done basic repairs to the roof and the exterior and had stripped rotten plaster off some interior walls to reveal bare brickwork. The rest was down to Evan. Slowly he began the process of making the space habitable, clearing the rubble and rubbish, knocking the concrete out of the windows and replacing it with plywood through which he cut holes to admit light, and eventually installing replacement sash windows.

*LEFT* The walls would have been plastered but many have now been stripped back to the old brickwork. Against this rough background of mottled colour and grainy texture, the natty 20th-century furnishings in the bedroom look extra sleek and sophisticated. The insert shows a detail of the ornate pressed-tin ceiling in the room now used as the kitchen.

*RIGHT* This school was built on a grand scale, with high ceilings, high windows and tall, glazed doorways. The entrance to Evan's first-floor apartment now leads to a corridor of sheetrock walls enclosing studios. Studied groupings of furniture, like this plastic moulded chair and table, are surrounded by space, giving them the look of exhibits in an art gallery.

Originally there must have been as many as six large classrooms and a room with a raised wooden floor at one end with the remains of a glazed partition dropping down from the ceiling to door height. About a year after Evan moved in an artist friend moved back to New York from London and decided to share the space and the restoration. The school had closed in the 1960s, and later internal walls had been inserted. Once these were down, leaving only six structural cast-iron columns and an area of slate flooring where the cloakrooms had been, they were free to divide their square feet into rooms.

The room with the raised floor became the kitchen, the slate floor marked out the boundaries of their new bathroom. The remaining space was divided by partition walls into three bedrooms, each the size of most New York City apartments, two spacious studios and a vast living room. All original features, such as the ornate pressed-tin ceiling in the kitchen, the chunky panelled doors

and the remains of glazed partitions were preserved and restored. The elaborate cast-iron staircase running down the back of the building was converted into a walk-in cupboard. New plaster walls were painted white and new plywood floors painted gloss grey-blue.

The architectural mix of new and old makes a pleasingly eccentric setting for Evan's collection of 20th-century furnishings. He now deals in these from his Williamsburg gallery, R 20th Century. 'I got into the business because I was interested in "found" objects and these were pieces you could find chucked out as junk before they became so fashionable. In a way this apartment was a found object – a found object you could live in.'

*LEFT* There are few visual clues that this handsome apartment was once a hat factory, with its wooden floor polished to such a sheen it reflects the furniture, its glazed internal doors, and its chic panelling to dado height.

*RIGHT* The magnificent hall with its stately staircase leading up from the 'winter' to the 'summer' apartment looks like the entrance to some grand, old English school or club. In truth, it is entirely the creation of Leitersdorf, the metal stair-rail recycled from the building's original 19th-century fire escape and the pressed-tin ceiling made especially for the space.

*ABOVE* One of the few references to the building's industrial past is the bare brickwork of the gently vaulted ceilings. In fact originally they were covered with a thick layer of plaster, but Leitersdorf decided he liked the look of the bricks and the raw edge they give to the interior. The glazing of the enormous windows is reflected in the design of the internal doors.

# hat trick

*Swiss architect Jonathan Leitersdorf does not measure his New York apartment in square feet, he measures it in acres: a quarter of an acre to be precise. In 1995 he bought a hat factory on Broadway built in 1894 as retail premises with workshops above. He put in new wiring, plumbing, windows and lifts and kept the tenth floor for himself, with its spectacular views from tall windows on four sides.*

As the roof was flat, he built another storey on top of the building. This gave him so much space that he decided to make each floor a self-contained unit, with its own kitchen and bathrooms. He calls the tenth floor his 'winter apartment' and the eleventh floor his 'summer apartment'.

*LEFT* Some of Leitersdorf's collection of clothing is housed in glamorous mahogany and glass cabinets once used for display in early 20th-century shops.

*RIGHT* In the master bedroom the plaster has been stripped off the brick walls and ceilings. Their rough, almost unfinished appearance is in striking counterpoint to the perfection of the polished floorboards and the beautifully restored original metal window frames. The doors into the room were salvaged from another old building in New York.

*BELOW* These intricately carved, antique double doors from India make a suitably magnificent entrance to the marble-lined master bathroom.

The upper floor, being all new, is a bright, white space with huge metal doors that swing open onto a garden complete with a mature ash tree, and the even more remarkable sight of a swimming pool. The inside is clean and cool, but from the outside the new structure is architecturally in keeping with the rest of the building, due to its sympathetic design and materials. The windows are metal framed with slim glazing bars and the bricks are reclaimed. 'The bricks cost a fortune,' Leitersdorf admits, 'but they are all slightly different colours and have a beautiful patina of age.'

While the interior of the summer apartment is contemporary, the winter one below has a distinctive vintage style. When Leitersdorf converted the building he retained as many of its features as possible, including some of the metal-framed windows and internal cast-iron pillars. The windows in his bedroom are 'lot' windows, an ingenious 19th-century invention of metal sashes counterbalanced by lead weights designed to melt in the event of a fire, thereby automatically shutting the windows and preventing the spread of the fire. These have been meticulously stripped and restored complete with all their brass fittings.

Also original are the gently vaulted ceilings, which have had four inches (ten centimetres) of plaster chipped away to reveal the old brickwork.

Some features have been adapted and cleverly recycled. The intricate metalwork of the old fire escape has been reused as banisters for the grand staircase, which links the two apartments. The remainder has been cut down to make balconettes for some of the windows, which Leitersdorf has extended to floor level. A more surprising example of recycling and adaptation is the swimming pool. 'A pool this size full of water weighs the equivalent of five extra storeys,' explains Leitersdorf, 'so it wouldn't normally be possible to install one on the roof of an old building. But this pool takes the place of the tanks for the original sprinkler system so is supported by a massive steel framework that was already in place.'

Other period features are new to the building. 'I wanted this space to have a 1920s, almost Bauhaus feel,' Leitersdorf explains. Bathrooms

*FAR LEFT* **The kitchen is another improbably glamorous room, its furnishings appearing to float on the glossy floor, punctuated by original cast-iron columns which have been painted shiny black. As elsewhere in the apartment, many of the fixtures and fittings are antique, including the huge pendant glass lights and the countertop glass cabinet.**

---

*ABOVE LEFT and ABOVE* **All the bathrooms have a strong vintage feel, and often contain reconditioned antique fittings. The brick-shaped tiles are new, but handmade, giving them an irregular, slightly aged look.**

---

*BELOW LEFT* **These kitchen cabinets and chunky china sink could have been lifted straight from an Edwardian country house. However, you can be certain that the plumbing is far from vintage in its power and efficiency.**

---

are lined with off-white, brick-shaped tiles. The fact that they are handmade and therefore slightly irregular makes them look antique. The hallway has a ceiling embellished with traditional pressed tin, from a Missouri company which has been making it for two hundred years.

Bathroom fittings are genuinely antique, sourced in Britain and France and refurbished. The glossy chestnut-brown floorboards were imported from the Netherlands, one set of double doors came from another old building in Manhattan, another intricately carved pair is from India. Even light fittings are antique, as is much of the furniture, including grand old glass and mahogany display cabinets, from Edwardian department stores, in which he keeps clothes.

The scale of this conversion is way beyond the budget of most of us. But Leitersdorf's respect for the fabric and style of the building, and his use of a mix of the reclaimed and handmade can equally be applied to square feet as opposed to acres.

The summer living room is a magnificent sixty feet (eighteen metres) long, occupying the whole of the first-floor space that was once the hayloft. The French doors, installed when the buildings were first converted, lead out onto a generous balcony. Outside, above the circular window, the remains of the original block and tackle, used to hoist the hay bales, is a reminder of the building's past life as a dairy barn. Inside, the smooth white walls make this a very sophisticated version of rustic living. Even the gingham upholstery is more urban than country due to its extra-large scale.

# dairy made

*Three round concrete silos guard the entrance to this country house on the coast of New York state. Windowless, and painted a vibrant rusty red with domed metal roofs, they huddle protectively next to the adjacent buildings like the towers of an alien castle. Emphasizing their role as sentinels, the main entrance to the house punches through the cylindrical walls of the middle silo, which has been planted with a small tree and shrubs to make an indoor circular courtyard. Inside the front door inner doors to right and left lead into the flanking silos, one of which is used as a wine cellar, the other as a boiler room.*

'I loved them from the moment I saw them,' says architect Zina Glazebrook. 'Fortunately my client agreed.' The silos are the dominant feature of a long, low group of buildings constructed in the 1930s as a dairy barn, quite separate from the farmhouse, which is further up the hill. The barn was in use until the 1960s (the original dairy housed about ninety cows), when the gentleman farmer who owned it sold it off with some land. In 1970 the buildings were converted to make a house, which was further extended in the 1980s. Although the conversion was not particularly sensitive, the silos remained intact.

*ABOVE LEFT* Like a magnified version of the round window in the hayloft, this giant porthole was salvaged from a courthouse in Toronto.

*ABOVE RIGHT* The front door is reached through one of the three silos that seem to guard the buildings like a trio of watchtowers. The wall lights were salvaged from another dairy farm.

*BELOW* The old pine floorboards in the hayloft have been restored and polished to a smooth finish.

LEFT and BELOW The ground-floor winter living room was converted from the long dairy barn and now has French doors and windows along both walls, opening on one side onto a covered veranda and terrace. The structural wooden beams have been painted white but still have a powerful architectural presence in the room, rising to a tall apex that magnifies the sense of space. Unpretentious furnishings mix modern upholstery with a recycled coffee table, a slightly primitive country cupboard and a traditional cane chair. The flooring is a natural matting, which looks stylish but also feels appropriately agricultural.

The dairy included a milking parlour, cowshed and hayloft. The construction was cast concrete and the roof was probably corrugated iron. When the owner bought the property much of the donkey work of transforming these unheated and largely windowless spaces into rooms fit for human as opposed to bovine inhabitation had already been done. The iron roof had been replaced with picturesque cedar shingles and there were plenty of windows. But the buildings had lost something of their gentle, agricultural atmosphere, a connection with the past that both architect and owner were keen to restore.

*FAR RIGHT* The architect Zina Glazebrook says she can feel the presence of the long-departed cows particularly strongly in the kitchen, an assertion that is hard to believe of a room so pristine. The main architectural link with the past is the floor, which is concrete, just as it was when the room was home to a dairy herd. However, this is concrete that has been polished to a silky sheen and which has had heating installed beneath it — a level of underfoot luxury alien to most cows.

Surfaces were carefully considered. Concrete was chosen for the kitchen floor. This is the same material the cows would once have clattered across, but refined to the smoothness of terrazzo by a process called 'power-trowelling', which beats it to a sheen. A further refinement was the installation of underfloor heating, banishing any hint of cold or damp. Upstairs the old pine floorboards of the hayloft, now the summer living room, have been scrubbed and polished and left bare. Structural roof beams in the winter living room are a reminder that this space was once a barn. Everything that could be saved or salvaged was used, including an old metal feeding trough, which has been planted with ferns.

Several of Zina's architectural additions came with their own history: a large round window once lit the interior of a courthouse in Toronto; a sliding door hanging from an industrial metal rail between the master bedroom and bathroom shut

the grain store of an upstate farm; metal wall lanterns in the entrance hall are from another old dairy. And, inspired by a feeding trough turned planter, Zina found another one and used it for the basin in the master bathroom.

One of the most dramatic transformations is the metamorphosis of milking parlour to sparkling indoor swimming pool. Zina painted the roof and walls white because she wanted it to have the feel of a wooden boathouse. Flowers and foliage planted outside the windows cast dappled shadows across the water as sunlight floods in.

Although the sea can only be glimpsed from upstairs rooms, it can always be heard. Timber decking and balconies, crisp white balustrading, and two outdoor showers, one tucked between the silos at first-floor level, the other conveniently placed between the terraces for washing off after the beach, give the house a perennially holiday feel. Inside, a uniform wash of white paint on walls, ceilings and woodwork ensures the sparsely furnished rooms are bright year round. The hot breath of the cows is a distant memory, but Zina thinks she has the aura of their gentle natures to thank for 'the peace and calm in the house'.

*ABOVE* An old grain-store door from a farm in upstate New York, hanging from its original metal rail, now divides the master bedroom and bathroom. Zina Glazebrook was at great pains not to eradicate the history of these buildings. Using recycled architectural features has helped to reintroduce the agricultural character that the previous conversion had so nearly banished.

*RIGHT* Looking from the bathroom to the bedroom, more creative recycling is apparent. The basin is an old lead-coated copper feeding trough.

*RIGHT* When Zina Glazebrook's client bought these old dairy buildings, they had already been converted. This long room with its sloping roof, where cows once stood in stalls to be milked, had been excavated to make a lap pool. However, its atmosphere was 'dank and sad'. Zina set about transforming it, inspired by her childhood in the Adirondacks. 'I wanted it to have the light, bright feel of an old boathouse, with that dappled sunshine you get in buildings near water.' Walls and roof are lined with planking, painted gloss white, and plants outside the windows cast moving shadows across the water. The windows at first-floor level give a view of the pool from the summer living room. At one end, an old feeding trough is hung on the wall as a planter, cascading with lacy ferns (not seen).

The façade of this apartment was once an opening for lorries. Now it is a front door next to a wall of window, which allows natural light into the otherwise windowless space. The kitchen units, *RIGHT and INSERT*, are the only fixed feature of an interior where furniture, and even pictures, are regularly rearranged. The horizontal grain of their wood and the glazing bars of the hand-blown opaque glass-fronted wall cabinets reflect the powerful lines of the buffers on the opposite wall.

# bay living

A loading bay is not the most obvious place to make a home. Designer Kenneth Hirst's apartment in the SoHo district of New York City was once the space where carts, and subsequently lorries, pulled in to deliver the raw materials to a factory making cardboard boxes. The building dates from the early 20th century. The brick walls inside the bay are lined between calf and chest level with a broad buffer of hefty horizontal beams designed to protect the walls, and the reversing lorries, from damage. To say these are distressed would be an understatement. Decades of bad driving have ensured that the timber is scored and scraped and comprehensively battered. The beams are also a signed work of art.

*ABOVE* The furnishings complement the strong architectural presence of the buffer beams. The dining chairs are wide and low and the wall-mounted CD player follows the rectangular pattern.

*FAR LEFT* At the far end of the apartment where the lorries used to back up, a mezzanine floor has been inserted just beyond the huge beams that supported the winch. The T-shaped structure hides utilities and shelters a small study. The bedroom, above, is surrounded by a low wall, giving it a view over the whole space.

*LEFT* The previous occupant, artist Carla Lavatelli, inscribed the buffer beams with words, signing them off as an artwork before she moved on.

Kenneth Hirst had been looking for a rooftop apartment when an estate agent persuaded him to look at this unusual property. Developed in 1976, as part of the SoHo artists in residence scheme, it was being occupied for three to four months of the year by an Italian sculptor, Carla Lavatelli. While she lived there, over the years, she inscribed single words, thoughts, and lines of poetry on the wood. Before she left, she signed the end of the beam. 'It's the most expensive work of art I ever bought,' laughs Kenneth.

The wall of bare brick and battered beams was not the only relic of the building's past. The opposite wall is new, and divides the original bay into two halves, but against its pristine white plaster towers a V-shaped structure of wood and metal, which once supported a massive winch in the middle of the loading bay. Again, the wood is split and dented and rough, studded with big metal bolts and braced with metal rods.

'The estate agent was right,' says Kenneth. 'As soon as I walked into the space I went "wow". It was such a dramatic volume and the beams made such a powerful and striking impact.' Guests have been echoing his reaction ever since. Thanks to imaginative lighting, furnishings and the addition of a mezzanine floor, this giant shoebox-shaped lorry park has been transformed into a handsome and practical space for living and entertaining.

Although the space had already been converted to residential use, Carla Lavatelli's cooking and bathing arrangements were far from sophisticated: a camping stove with two hotplates, and a tiny bathroom. The mezzanine floor had already been installed at the far end of the space, like two boxes stacked one on top of the other within the bigger box of the apartment. The smaller box underneath hides the boiler, other utilities and storage. Upstairs the bedroom is on a platform surrounded by a low wall while the bathroom is enclosed and screened by internal windows of translucent 'rice-paper' glass. Here there is very little natural light but Kenneth has compensated using a series of warm, adjustable light sources, including track lighting and table lamps.

Loading bays do not generally require windows and this apartment has only one, albeit a big one. The entrance to the bay has been turned into a wall of window but every other wall is blank. Kenneth Hirst has turned these expanses of wall to design advantage, not by peppering them with pictures, which he prefers to prop on the floor, but by emphasizing the dramatic horizontal 'woodscape' of the beams. The kitchen units, in pale anigre wood, are made so that the grain runs horizontally, the wall cupboards have doors divided into three long rectangles, and even the wall-mounted stereo takes up the theme.

He also takes full advantage of the uninterrupted floor space. The kitchen is the only fixed element, with its central counter and a big

*ABOVE* A sofa tucks snugly against the low wall that surrounds the bedroom at first-floor level. Throughout the apartment there are interesting contrasts between the refinement of some of the architectural additions and the rough-and-ready nature of existing features. No attempt has been made to hide pipework, which is painted bright white to match the walls and ceiling.

*RIGHT* Very little daylight from the wall of window reaches the back of the apartment. In the ground-floor utility room and in the first-floor bathroom artificial light is a necessity throughout the day. Here, hidden light sources turn necessity to dramatic effect.

*FAR RIGHT* The open bedroom with its view over the apartment is divided from the bathroom by the line of an old beam. Internal windows are made from glass layered with rice paper, providing a translucent screen that filters light and affords some privacy.

*LEFT* **The massive slabs of timber that supported the winch are studded with bolts, cracked and dented by years of use. The slim lines of the glazing bars on the upstairs windows look all the more dainty in their rugged company.**

wooden cabinet within which slot the fridge, oven and microwave. Everything else gets moved around and even set at different angles. As a counterpoint to the straight lines, Kenneth uses his ever-expanding collection of shells to make curvaceous displays of what he calls 'the most beautiful architectural forms on the planet'.

*THIS PAGE* The owners of this glossy London conversion bought apartments on two floors as shells. They employed architect Ben Kelly to fit out the space because they felt confident that he would retain the 'industrial edge' that first attracted them. The interplay between the rough concrete carcass of the building and the polish of Kelly's additions provides much of the visual interest.

*RIGHT* The uppermost of the two apartments is sited on a corner of the building, with windows and a balcony on two sides giving panoramic views over Central London towards St Paul's Cathedral in one direction and the tower of Centrepoint in the other. This level was the obvious choice for the living room, and the principal seating area takes full advantage of the city panorama. The L-shaped sofa neatly echoes the right angle where the two walls of window meet.

# shoe shine

An old shoe factory sounds like a
quirky, even a rather attractive place,
all rows of cobblers' benches and the
lingering scent of sweet, new leather.
When a film producer and art director
first visited the building that was to
become their London home, it was
anything but attractive. This space
had originally housed offices and light
manufacturing for Dr Scholl shoes, but
gutted and ready for redevelopment as
'loft-style' apartments it was more
like a multi-storey car park.

'It took a quantum leap of faith and imagination to believe that it
could ever make a liveable space,' remember the owners. 'It's a
1930s concrete building, and we liked that industrial aesthetic,
but we didn't want an apartment that felt too austere or ultra-
minimalist.' What the building lacked in architectural charm it
made up for in location. They were able to buy two units on the
fifth and sixth floors which, while not directly one above the other,
overlapped sufficiently to build a linking staircase. The upper floor
is on a corner of the building, with windows and a balcony on two
sides and magnificent views of the city looking south towards
St Paul's Cathedral and west to Centrepoint.

They bought the apartments as shells and chose Ben Kelly as
their architect. Best known for his stark, cutting-edge design for
the Hacienda nightclub in Manchester, this was a rare venture into
domestic design for him. 'We wanted a designer who would retain
the integrity of the space but also introduce some sensuality,' say the
owners. 'We felt Ben Kelly would be sympathetic to the building's
origins as a work space and would ensure it didn't lose that edge.'

The industrial aesthetic is appropriately softened in the bedroom, where birch-clad plywood panels the wall behind the bed and continues round at a right angle where it lines the back of a wall of cupboards. These cupboards form one wall of a corridor, which leads from the entrance to the bedroom. When the door is shut, *INSERT ABOVE*, the full-length mirror transforms the space into a compact dressing room.

*INSERT BELOW* The bath is separated from the bedroom by a low wall and a bench over a radiator, and has been positioned to make the most of the view. Other bathroom facilities are modestly screened behind translucent acid-etched glass panels.

Their first and least difficult decision was to use the upper floor as their main living space in order to take full advantage of the views. The lower level is divided by partition walls into a large master bedroom with an open-plan bathroom, a guest bedroom and office space, a utility room, and a downstairs cloakroom. The upper floor is open-plan, loosely divided into an expansive seating area, a dining area and a kitchen. The only interruption to the flow of floor space is a central floor-to-ceiling L-shaped unit, which provides storage and open shelving.

The 'industrial aesthetic' which first attracted them has been preserved in the raw exposed concrete of the ceilings and beams with their rough, mottled patina. According to Ben Kelly one of the main problems of converting commercial and industrial spaces into workable, practical homes is how to deal with services. 'When you have a monolithic structure like this,' he explains, 'there are only certain routes for the gas, water and electricity.' Sometimes these constraints can affect where bathrooms and kitchens are placed. In this instance they were lucky and their chosen layout was workable.

Underfloor heating ensures there are no radiators and very few visible pipes. Where pipes are on show, leading from the oven extractor fan, for example, they are encased in shiny steel and become an architectural feature. Similarly all the electrical wiring is surface-mounted, neatly housed in metal casings criss-crossing the ceiling and in places running up the concrete supporting beams, which have also been left unpainted. In contrast, the floors, shelving, bedroom and kitchen cupboards are natural wood in warm, glossy shades from pale honey to dark toffee.

'Playing off' the concrete carcass of the building's structure against sophisticated and glamorous materials such as glass, polished wood, stainless steel, and the snowy white plaster of the walls is a theme throughout the apartment. Floors are in merbau, which has a rich auburn glow, stair treads are American cherry, and the bedroom cupboards and wall panelling are birch-faced plywood. The introduction of so much wood, and the softness of fabrics on the sofas and cushions, has provided the sensuality the owners sought for their interior. The industrial edge has been softened, but there is enough raw concrete to ensure it is far from forgotten.

*ABOVE* This old school was originally a single-storey building with two classrooms, which had ceilings reaching up into the apex of the roof. When it was converted to make a house, the space was divided laterally to make bedrooms upstairs under the steep point of the eaves. Mark Smith added tongue-and-groove panelling cupboards in this bedroom in the triangular space where the roof slopes to the floor.

*LEFT* The addition of an upstairs has given the downstairs rooms relatively low ceilings, but Mark minimized the effect by painting the joists the same pale colours as the walls. Traditional sofas and chairs are upholstered in plain, natural fabrics and the primitive coffee table is an old pig bench, its gory past now a distant memory.

# homework

*After the 1870 School Act, which required all children to attend school, gabled Victorian gothic schoolhouses sprang up in almost every English village. Most comprised a couple of classrooms with lofty ceilings and windows placed too high for pupils to be distracted by a view of anything other than sky. As the village school has declined these buildings have often been adopted as homes, although the dour, churchy architecture designed to keep children's noses to their slates does not necessarily lend itself to a comfortable family house.*

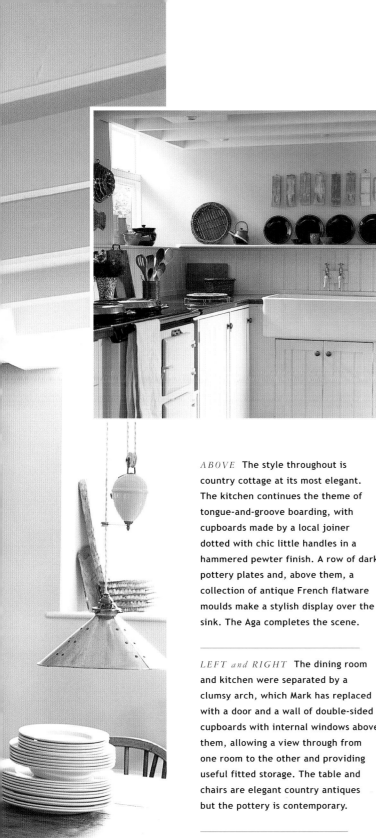

*ABOVE* The style throughout is country cottage at its most elegant. The kitchen continues the theme of tongue-and-groove boarding, with cupboards made by a local joiner dotted with chic little handles in a hammered pewter finish. A row of dark pottery plates and, above them, a collection of antique French flatware moulds make a stylish display over the sink. The Aga completes the scene.

*LEFT and RIGHT* The dining room and kitchen were separated by a clumsy arch, which Mark has replaced with a door and a wall of double-sided cupboards with internal windows above them, allowing a view through from one room to the other and providing useful fitted storage. The table and chairs are elegant country antiques but the pottery is contemporary.

*FAR RIGHT* Looking from the dining room through to the living room, the 18th-century painted dresser on the right holds a dinner service commissioned from local potter David Garland. The floor is the original terracotta tiles, worn to a smooth, rosy glow by the patter of tiny feet. Over it Mark has laid flat-weave rugs from Roger Oates.

Mark Smith's Cotswold cottage was built as a 'dame school' and has converted to a life of cosy domesticity better than most. This is partly because it pre-dates the Victorian architectural pattern, being at least two hundred years old, first appearing in the records in 1813. Dame schools were charitable institutions set up to teach basic literacy and Bible reading to poor children. They were run by spinsters or housewives of the village, hence their title.

When Mark bought the building it had already been converted to make a small house. A floor had been added, halving the height of the old classrooms to create bedrooms in the steep gable of the roof, and the larger of the two classrooms had been split by a wall and a clumsy arch to make a living and dining room. A few tell-tale original features remained: a wood-burning stove, which can only have provided meagre warmth in the double-height space; the attractively worn quarry tile flooring; and the narrow double doors, which were one of the entrances to the school.

Mark's structural changes are so in keeping it is hard now to guess where the old stops and the new begins. He gained another downstairs reception room by rebuilding a sloping extension on the footprint of the old lean-to coal store. He also rebuilt the wall that separates the living and dining rooms using a glazed partition above double-sided cupboards, providing extra light, views through the interior and storage space, all in one neat design solution. In the living room he removed a window seat and discovered quarry tiling running beneath to what was once the threshold of a double door. He reinstated the doors such that this room also opens into the garden.

Some of the changes were purely practical. The windows, for example, were replaced with new, double-glazed wooden frames, which look entirely appropriate to the age of the building and provide excellent insulation. The tongue-and-groove panelling that lines some of the walls was an aesthetic choice. It adds to the feel of rustic simplicity and gives the interior a pleasing cohesion as all the

new joinery, including internal doors and fitted cupboards in the kitchen and dining room, is also made with tongue and groove.

Mark wanted to keep the decoration of his country retreat as simple as possible. He achieved this by using pale, neutral colours throughout, covering the dark wood stain of the ceiling joists with a thin coat of emulsion and lightening the whole effect. There is an emphasis on natural materials and on plain, traditional design, with a butler's sink and an Aga in the kitchen. The deep sofa in the living room is covered in canvas and the curtains are unlined sacking.

Mixed in with the country antiques are bold, modern table lamps and the contemporary ceramics that are one of Mark's passions. The overall effect is unpretentious, gently modern, and a lot warmer in winter than when children sat in rows chanting their catechisms.

*ABOVE* A lean-to coal shed has been transformed to make a light and airy 'garden room', which leads off the kitchen. This room and the kitchen open straight onto the sheltered stone paved terrace, the perfect setting for informal summer entertaining.

*RIGHT* In the main bedroom, tucked under the eaves, the bed is placed centrally against the windows to make the most of the limited ceiling height. Woven fabrics in stripes and checks keep the effect simple but cosy.

# recycled spaces furniture and lighting

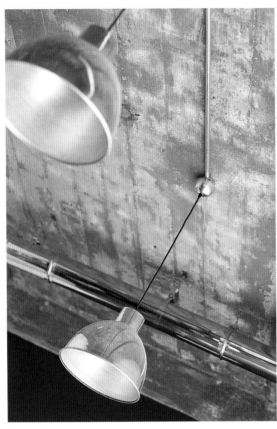

One of the attractions of reusing a building originally designed as a school or a warehouse is the allure of wide-open floor space. Old buildings designed to be lived in are generally divided into spaces small enough to be warmed by the heat from a single open fire. Lofty drawing rooms were for the wealthy and for show. Otherwise, as soon as the cold weather began, it was far more comfortable to be ensconced in a room of modest proportions with heavy curtains and a good blaze warming the walls.

Efficient insulation and central heating mean that today we can enjoy the physical freedom and the aesthetics of big indoor spaces without the winter discomfort. Most people who buy a warehouse or factory conversion are keen to preserve the sense of space and opt for open-plan living. Space also gives you freedom to move furniture around, to choose enormous pieces that couldn't be squeezed into an ordinary room, to be playful and experimental.

RECYCLED SPACES suit recycled furnishings — old plush cinema seats for armchairs, chapel chairs for dining chairs, a chemist's cabinet for storing glasses. Mark Smith has a pig bench as a coffee table. Jonathan Leitersdorf keeps clothes in antique department-store display cases.

MIX THE OLD AND THE NEW with impunity. You probably have enough space to keep them apart if necessary.

BIG SPACES are exhilarating but sometimes need breaking up. Free-standing storage units, as in architect Ben Kelly's conversion of the shoe factory, make attractive and useful room dividers.

FURNITURE IN MOTION. Kenneth Hirst regularly rearranges his furniture. Make the moving easier by putting wheels on heavier pieces. Wheels with integral brakes, as on hospital trolleys, are ideal.

SCREENS, once designed as protection from draughts, come in all shapes and sizes, antique or contemporary, and are a flexible means of providing a little privacy or enclosure.

BUILDINGS always retain an aura of their past. Most people want to preserve as much of the original fabric of a converted building as practical, but you can also refer to its past through its furnishings. Zina Glazebrook made a basin for her client from an old feeding trough and used another as a planter in buildings that were once a dairy.

ARCHITECTURAL SALVAGE yards often contain items too unwieldy or bizarre to be incorporated in your average house, whether a giant bath or fittings from an Edwardian pub. Keep an open mind and be inspired.

LESS IS MORE. Sometimes the less you do, the better the effect. If you buy a battered piece of furniture, ripe for restoration, consider leaving it as it is. Chipped paint and chewed edges look good against bare brick.

THE INDUSTRIAL AESTHETIC is attractively raw but too much bare concrete and stainless steel can end up feeling cold and brutal. A home also needs comfort and some luxury.

BIG SPACES often have high ceilings. Make sure pendant lights are bold in scale and hang low enough not to feel like factory lighting.

WIRING can be wall-mounted if your building has a concrete shell. Make a feature of the metal wire casings for real industrial credibility.

IF YOU HAVE an acreage of wooden flooring, consider installing floor-mounted electric sockets at strategic points to avoid trailing wires.

# recycled spaces fabric and finishing touches

When you choose to live in a space that once housed machinery, or offices, or ranks of school desks or even lorries, you have to work extra hard to make it feel like a home. The proportions of the rooms will not be domestic, walls and ceilings may be bare concrete, windows may be intimidatingly large and high. If you are converting a barn or an agricultural building there may be no windows at all. Somehow you have to make this place feel like a retreat from work, not a place of work.

Fabrics are important in any domestic interior, bringing softness and comfort, both visual and physical. Rooms without fabrics lack intimacy and warmth. Even a bathroom looks a little too monastic and clinical without a fat, fluffy towel hanging somewhere. In an ex-industrial space fabrics are even more important than usual.

The same applies to all the finishing touches that add character and individuality to an interior. You may prefer a very spare interior, like Kenneth Hirst's, but unless you are going for out-and-out minimalism you still need to incorporate elements that speak of your own history and personality. Kenneth Hirst inherited a hugely personal artwork in the shape of the buffer beams covered with graffiti documenting the highs and lows of the life of the artist who lived there before him, but has added evidence of one of his own private passions with displays of the shells he collects.

BIG SPACES can take vibrant colour. Upholster individual pieces of furniture in glowing orange, pillar-box red, or intense jade green for powerful accents that will warm up a space and attract the eye.

BIG SPACES can equally absorb punchy pattern. A mild chintz or a pretty sprig would look lost in all the interiors on the previous pages, with the exception of Mark Smith's home, which has cottagey proportions.

CONTEMPORARY FABRIC designs look better than traditional ones for the same reason. Even classic stripes and checks need to be magnified to make an impact, as in the living rooms of the old dairy.

WHEN USING PLAIN fabrics, pay extra attention to texture.

CONSIDER using unusual items that have relevance to a building's past as decorative additions. Zina Glazebrook hung a pair of spades, once used for mucking out, in the entrance hall of the old dairy, where they look as much like sculptural artworks as tools.

HUGE WINDOWS can be prohibitively costly to curtain. Cheap and good-looking options include linen scrim, more usually used for window-cleaning cloths, which makes an excellent coarse semi-sheer, and artist's canvas, which comes in differing weights, the heaviest of which hangs particularly well.

BLINDS use a fraction of the amount of material as curtains.

ARCHITECTURAL SALVAGE yards are just as good for finding decorative items as furnishings, especially if you have space to accommodate the oversized. Jonathan Leitersdorf has part of an old advertising display for Shell petrol on top of his bedroom cupboard and Evan Snyderman has a disco ball hanging from his ceiling.

PICTURES need to be big enough to get noticed. Framing old posters and blowing up black-and-white photographs are options.

IF YOU WANT to display small things in a big space, group them tightly to give a more substantial effect.

# COUNTRY HOUSE

Classic country-house style requires a buxom sofa or two, several acres of faded chintz and a brace of Labrador. In which case none of the following houses qualify. Instead we have French chic in a farmhouse, chintz with a twist in an urban terrace, and funky wallpaper in a rural rectory. The closest we come to buxom sofas is in London's East End, which only goes to show that country-house style has moved on since the days of the regulation Labrador and that you don't even have to live in the country to enjoy it.

*ABOVE* The doors and pediment from an antique armoire have been used to make a cupboard, set into the thickness of the walls in a corner of the living room. The original rubbed, grey paintwork is complemented by the unbleached antique linen of the sofa cover and cushions.

*RIGHT* On the other side of the same room the deep walls form a niche for built-in seating. A generous padding of cushions, also covered in unbleached linen, makes this an inviting corner for curling up with a good book, or an afternoon nap. Fabrics, walls, furniture and the traditional terracotta tiles of the floor make a palette of gentle, neutral colour against which the dark gloss of the gilt-framed oil paintings is thrown into rich relief.

*LEFT* It is hard to imagine when this, the 'grand salon', was a sheep-shed and fruit store. The uneven walls and the rough old beams are original but the reclaimed terracotta floor and the antique panelling are new to the room.

# farmhouse chic

*French country style is an alluring combination of the earthy and the elegant. The unbleached linens and monochrome toiles, the wooden furniture with its chalky rubbed paintwork, the floors in stone and terracotta tiles, the white tin-glazed pottery, the ironwork: all have the look of things that might have been made locally, using materials quarried or grown or fashioned from the land. Like the produce in the local markets, these are furnishings that seem to embody the flavour of the countryside itself.*

Mireille and Jean-Claude Lothon's Normandy house has just this feel of being part of the landscape. Built in the 10th century as a farmhouse in an ancient village, it is surrounded by low walls topped by a little roof of old clay tiles, giving it, as Mireille puts

*LEFT and RIGHT* These rooms, in the past home to five cows, are now the kitchen and breakfast room. The floor is on two levels and divided by a low wall with a row of old beams rising up to support the roof. Clever and practical use has been made of this original feature; the broad top of the wall is stacked with crockery, the pretty cream plates, tureens and bowls that are used every day. Cutlery sits in pots. The arrangement is attractive and convenient. Again, pieces of old panelling from antique furniture have been used to make kitchen cupboards, while further storage is contained in slots and niches cut into the low wall. Even the wall cupboards have old doors. Behind the vertical beams there are linen Roman blinds, which can be lowered to make a division between the dining and kitchen areas.

it, 'a feeling of peace and intimacy'. The casement windows are prettily shuttered and the proportions are modest and charming; 'so charming,' says Mireille, 'that the instant we saw it we wanted to buy it.'

Initially, the house was a country retreat for Mireille, Jean-Claude and their four children, somewhere quiet, remote and old-fashioned to escape to at weekends from their main house in the Parisian suburb of Versailles. Fifteen years ago they made it their principal home. Jean-Claude left his job and joined Mireille's antiques business. And now two of their grown-up daughters, Mathilde and Alice, also collaborate, exercising their artistic skills creating paint finishes with a soft patina of use, for the French country furniture that is their parents' speciality.

The house dates from a time when farmers were largely self-sufficient. There are nine ground-floor rooms, only four of which were living quarters. The kitchen still had its pretty wall and floor tiling, cream and terracotta diamonds on the floor and a smaller harlequin of black and white where the sink once stood. Although this space is now a living room the tiles have been left intact as an attractive reminder of the room's original use.

The remaining ground-floor rooms were a fruit store, a sheep-shed, a cowshed, a stable, and a laundry. Two barns complete the complex of buildings around the original cobbled farmyard. Mireille and Jean-Claude took out the low, wooden ceiling above the sheep-shed and the adjacent fruit store and transformed the space into their 'grand salon'. The cowshed became the kitchen and the haylofts bedrooms, each with an integral bathroom. Wiring, plumbing and central heating were installed

*LEFT* A charming oval window and a strip of chequerboard wall tiles mark the position of the old kitchen sink in the original farmhouse kitchen, now a living room. The cream and terracotta floor tiles are also original. By leaving intact so many relics of the building's past, and using old materials wherever possible, the Lothons have preserved its sense of history even though they are occupying the spaces in a new way.

*RIGHT* The hayloft, with its steep roof and toffee-coloured beams, has been divided to make bedrooms and bathrooms. A traditional French quilted 'boutis' covers the bed and the curtain tie-backs are strips of toile de Jouy.

and the metamorphosis from humble peasant farm to spacious modern home was complete.

Much of the charm of the interior is due to the careful way Mireille and Jean-Claude have retained the original fabric of the building wherever possible. Just as tiles have been saved in the old kitchen, so in the new one the upright beams that divided the cowshed still stand in an irregular, crooked row between a low wall and the ceiling. More than a quaint feature, they are integral to the design of the room, forming a rustic room divider between the eating and cooking areas.

Upstairs in the attic bedrooms, the oak beams of the old hayloft form their own handsome geometry, highlighted by plain white walls, while downstairs the rough old ceiling beams have been painted white for a slightly more formal look. Where there were original floors they have been kept, while traditional terracotta floor tiles have replaced trodden earth in the former animal sheds.

Thanks to their trade in antique and second-hand French country furniture Mireille and Jean-Claude have been able to do some creative recycling. The dining room has a moveable panelled wall made up of doors from a dismantled armoire, behind which are bookshelves. In other rooms panelled doors from other pieces of dilapidated antique furniture have been used to create cupboards built into the walls. Even new pieces of furniture are given a patina of age thanks to skilfully applied layers of paint, and the finished effect is of an interior that has been lived in and loved, but little changed for generations.

*ABOVE* The first floor of this small 1740s terraced house would once have been divided into two rooms at front and back and a tiny landing where the staircase turned up to the next floor. When Helen Ellery bought the house it was being used as a salvage yard and most internal partitions had been ripped out. This allowed her to make a semi-open-plan arrangement of sitting room at the front, with a kitchen at the back and a dining area in between.

*RIGHT* Helen reinstated the hallway to make separate office space on the ground floor and in the basement. A strip of grass-green carpet leads upstairs from work to home.

*LEFT* The sitting room contains only two pieces of furniture, both on a grand scale. The antique cupboard provides masses of storage and the sofa ample seating. Even the curtains are big, floor length and generously gathered. Interestingly, the effect is to make the room seem more comfortably capacious than cramped.

# organic conversion

*Helen Ellery had long admired her house from the outside before it came up for sale. Part of a row of mid-18th-century shops in a quiet London street, it was being used as a reclamation yard. Internally it had been stripped to make space for stock, but it offered Helen the opportunity to live above her interior design business.*

Like so many old London houses squeezed onto narrow plots, the rooms are stacked one on top of the other. For the modern family inhabiting the basement and attics as well as the floors in between, the endless stairs of a typical terraced house are a nuisance, albeit a healthy one. But in this instance the layout worked; two floors for work, two

for home. Fortunately, because the house had already been gutted, Helen was free to rearrange internal walls. This allowed her to add a hallway in the ground floor, which had previously been a single shop space, and to leave the first floor open-plan.

'I wanted to maintain as strict a separation between work and home as possible,' she explains. The front door opens onto a strip of grass-green carpet, which leads upstairs like a garden path towards the light of the stairwell window. If you take the path up and turn the corner you find yourself facing a small dining area, with a kitchen to the left and ahead the roomy sofa that presides over the diminutive front living room.

Before the walls came down this whole area would have been divided into a front room and a tiny back room opening off a square of landing. Helen discovered that in its long history the house had also been a tripe merchant's and a hosiery store so it is very probable that previous owners, also living above the shop, used these rooms as a parlour and possibly a bedroom. A short section of wall dividing the kitchen from the living area is the only reminder of this older arrangement of rooms.

On the floor above Helen has managed to retain the two bedrooms and add a bathroom by walling off a thin strip of landing space, which now houses a bath and shower, tiny basin and even a lavatory. Counteracting potential claustrophobia, she has raised the ceilings of these rooms into the roof space, and opened up views of sky

*TOP and RIGHT* The kitchen area is separated from the living room by a peninsula of wall and from the dining area by nothing more than a change from floorboards to a chequerboard of black-and-white tiles, which looks like a much grander floor seen through the wrong end of a telescope.

*ABOVE LEFT and RIGHT* At the top of the stairs in the pocket of space that would once have been the landing, Helen has placed a table and chairs overlooked by a very large clock. This section of staircase is original but the windows, which Helen also stripped back to the wood to match the stairs, are 19th as opposed to 18th century.

*TOP* Upstairs are two little bedrooms and an even littler bathroom. Helen made the most of the second bedroom by building a bed on a platform, which extends over the tiny fireplace. Beneath are storage cupboards, which help make up for the attic space lost when she extended the ceilings of these rooms into the roof.

*ABOVE* Fitted cupboards maximize storage space. The wardrobe in the main bedroom tucks into a corner.

through two skylight windows, one above the bathroom, one above the stairwell.

As for period features, Helen has retained and nurtured those remaining, stripping the original upper portion of staircase and the window frames back to the natural wood, and topping the brick fireplace in the living room, which had lost its surround, with a simple wooden mantel. She has also added features; tongue-and-groove panelling lining walls and ceilings, reclaimed pine doors and reclaimed pine floorboards.

The decorative theme of the house was inspired by Helen's love of gardens and the countryside where she was brought up. 'When I first came to work in London I never thought it could feel like home, but here I have managed to create a little sanctuary.' The scheme takes its cue from nature, using earthy shades of brown and terracotta downstairs, moving up through paler neutrals in the first-floor living space, towards the duck-egg blue of a light summer sky in the bedrooms, where flowery fabrics burst into bloom on the bedroom curtains and the stairwell window blind.

This is not country-house style in the classic sense, but a pared-down, modernized version, mixing pieces of antique furniture such as the enormous wall-to-wall cabinet in the living room with paintings by contemporary artists, and using chintzy designs against plain walls. The effect is fresh and contemporary, but with a cosy atmosphere.

*ABOVE and RIGHT* Helen managed to squeeze a bathroom onto her landing. The bath is the exact width of the room and the walls have been tiled from floor to ceiling so that it can double as a shower.

*LEFT* Nostalgia is an important element of her home for Helen Ellery. She says her bedroom reminds her of Enid Blyton stories, with its vintage wooden bed, old-fashioned quilt and blankets and flowery curtains.

*LEFT*  In a room with soaring ceilings and ornate cornices, potential pomposity is deflated by the addition of quirky contemporary artworks and a child's Noah's ark. Beyond the cut-out trees by 1960s artist Mo McDermott are real trees and a collection of painted metal toadstools, which once graced a children's television programme.

*RIGHT*  Unusual vintage fabrics cover an inherited giltwood sofa and its cushions, giving a contemporary twist to a grand antique. Using a modern fabric on old furniture can make the conventional look surprising and fresh.

# country fashion

*When an ex-fashion editor decamps from the city to a Georgian rectory deep in the countryside, you can expect an interesting decorating fusion. From the outside, Cosmo Fry and Lulu Anderson's house is the very image of the conventional rural idyll, all honey-coloured stone and gracious sash windows, surrounded by trees and fields. But the moment you step through the front door you find yourself in rooms that are far from conformist.*

Cosmo Fry bought The Old Rectory twenty five years ago, when it was badly in need of repair. A fire had almost completely gutted the interior in the 1920s and destroyed the third storey, which has never been replaced. The 1760s staircase was lost and only the drawing room was left with plaster cornice and marble chimney piece intact.

*ABOVE LEFT and RIGHT* **Installed twenty years ago, the simple white Formica kitchen made by Cosmo Fry's company, Countertops, has stood the test of time. The table is from a haberdasher's shop, its old glass top now replaced by more Formica. Adorning the walls are late Victorian and Edwardian enamel advertisements for Fry's chocolate, the business once owned by Cosmo's family.**

*RIGHT* **The bold monochrome wallpaper by Neisha Crosland brings a flourish of contemporary style to the bright, white entrance hall. The unusual table lamp with its fibre-optic innards dates from the 1960s.**

The layout of rooms, however, remained largely unchanged, although it is not certain where the kitchens and domestic offices were originally placed. All the ground-floor rooms, the drawing room, kitchen and hall at the front of the house, and the playroom, snooker room and study at the back, are grandly proportioned, with high ceilings and tall windows. The only structural change made by Cosmo was upstairs, where he knocked a door through from the main bedroom to an adjacent smaller room to make an en suite bathroom. Another bedroom was converted into a third bathroom.

The use of rooms downstairs was also adjusted. The room that is now Cosmo's study was once the morning room, so called because it was where the mistress of the house would undertake her morning tasks of correspondence and liaison with the head servants about cooking and other household business. The room now used as a snooker room was probably once the dining room. Cosmo Fry and Lulu Anderson entertain generously but informally, thinking nothing of twenty adults and nineteen children for lunch. 'In summer we set up a trestle table in Cosmo's office, which opens onto the garden,' says Lulu. 'Either that or we eat in the kitchen. We wouldn't use a grand dining room.'

Their informal style of entertaining is reflected in the way they have furnished these potentially pompous rooms. The generous hall is bright and bold, with white paint and wallpaper in a striking design by Neisha Crosland. Lulu runs a small boutique at nearby Babington House, its thoroughly urban contents displayed in a rustic summerhouse in the grounds. 'I stock many of Neisha's designs,' she explains, 'so I live with them at work and didn't feel daunted by putting them up on my walls at home, even though they are large scale and very contemporary.'

Furnishings in the hall are a foretaste of things to come, with a funky 1960s glass lamp complete with fibre-optic innards on an antique table, above which hangs a large gilt-framed oil painting. The mix of the fine with the amusing, the expected with the surprising, and the antique with the vintage, nearly new and new, continues in the drawing room, where old chairs are covered in unusual 1950s fabrics and a tall cut-out sculpture of trees from the 1960s stands in front of the leafy view.

Cosmo has collected contemporary art all his adult life, taking his cue from his father, also a collector and patron of the arts, and

ABOVE LEFT Some of Cosmo Fry's extensive collection of works by contemporary and 20th-century artists hangs on the wall of his study. Here, as elsewhere in the house, inherited antique furniture from the 18th and 19th centuries cohabits with much more recent pieces, in this case a streamlined cabinet from the 1950s.

ABOVE RIGHT In a room where all the art, and some of the furnishings, has a distinctly modern character, the boxy profile of this inlaid Biedermeier sofa looks entirely in keeping, despite being designed two hundred years ago.

RIGHT The main bedroom has a shag-pile carpet and a shaggy rug from IKEA to match, staple-gunned onto the bedhead, INSERT.

buying works direct from the artist. He also collects old advertisements for Fry's chocolate, once the family firm. Enamel plaques emblazoned with his surname adorn the kitchen walls, while the kitchen units in streamlined white Formica were made by his own company, Countertops, which manufactures laminate furniture. Formica appears in other guises in the house, from furniture to picture frames, and is the decorative leitmotif of the trendily cheap and cheerful Cardiff hotel, The Big Sleep, that is another of the couple's business ventures.

Upstairs there is more bold wallpaper, and bedrooms where vintage lamps sit next to antique beds. The comfort and scale are classic country house, but the modern art and retro furnishings make it newly fresh and fashionable.

*LEFT and ABOVE* **According to Lulu this bedroom had a heavy Victorian feel, dominated by the antique half-tester bed and rich red drapes. Another bold wallpaper from Neisha Crosland was the perfect antidote. Also added were large-scale vintage and contemporary table lamps, a striking curtain lining that picks up the circular motif of the wallpaper, and a painting by contemporary artist Craigie Aitchison. The result is an arresting fusion of tradition and innovation and far from either heavy or Victorian.**

The interior of the house had been stripped out over the years, giving the architect an unusual freedom to redesign the layout and architectural detail. All the panelling is new, made in MDF and painted.

*LEFT and RIGHT* The reception rooms on the raised ground floor form an L-shape around the staircase, which rises to the right of the front door. The longer leg of the L is the double drawing room, which spans the back of the house, and the shorter is the dining room, which looks out over the street. Instead of panelling, the dining room has a gorgeous multi-coloured chinoiserie wallpaper complete with dancing figures and dwarf tigers.

# inconspicuous consumption

*A hundred years ago Adrian and Belinda Hull's elegant early 18th-century townhouse was being used as a consumption clinic. There are still wooden pavilions at the back, on land that no longer belongs to the house, where patients were nursed. Then it was a foot clinic, then a birth-control clinic. When they bought the house from the council there were basins in every room and a litter of rubber gloves, coffee cups, leaflets and other less salubrious health-care detritus.*

There was also what their architect Gus Alexander calls 'a lot of Edwardian cupboardry', presumably for storing all those cork-stoppered bottles of medicaments, a basement dispensary with a little window and a shelf like an old-fashioned ticket office, and a dumb waiter to minimize the journeys a nurse might have to make from dispensary and kitchens to patients on the three floors above. The only original feature was the staircase, which runs at a right angle to the front door, rising past the front windows and giving the house a particularly spacious feel as you enter.

The house was first built in 1705, promptly burnt down, then rebuilt in 1706 as a comfortable middle class home in the comfortable middle class East End of London. Some hundred years later the area began to decline as the wealthy were driven west by the increasingly unpleasant smoke from growing industrialization. Today they are

ABOVE Matching fireplaces face one another across the length of the drawing room, one end of which is filled by a grand piano, the other by sofas and a leather armchair. Cushions in rich colours and fabrics glow against the background of neutral paint.

slowly returning (Adrian is a banker), reclaiming houses like this one, which have been used as offices or divided into flats, and turning them back into family homes.

Because of its date the house is listed. Although its owners would have liked to change the 19th-century four-paned sash windows back to their pattern of early Georgian glazing bars, they were not allowed to. But the Victorians did them one favour by extending the house laterally, filling in a gap where carriages once passed through to stables at the back and making the house a generous and unusual five bays wide. This and the staircase, and Gus Alexander's enthusiasm, persuaded the Hulls that it was a house well worth rescuing.

Because the house had been so comprehensively altered internally, there was a certain amount of freedom when re-establishing the room layouts. They decided to keep the lower ground floor as a kitchen. A modern Aga takes the place of a range, and sleek limestone flooring is the contemporary equivalent of flagstones. Kitchen cupboards are painted wood and their design echoes the plain fielded panels of an old fitted cupboard next to the Aga. The smaller adjacent rooms that would once have been a scullery, pantry and storeroom are now a larder with thick oak shelving, a laundry and a cloakroom. The Edwardian 'cupboardry' has been retained, as has the dumb waiter and the old dispensary, its small shelf now more likely to hold bottles of wine.

*ABOVE* The wide staircase with its shallow treads and prettily turned banisters was the only original feature that remained intact. Built against the front façade of the house, it rises to the first-floor bedrooms past a tall sash window, which floods it with light.

*ABOVE* **The main bedroom is on the first floor, at the back of the house overlooking the garden. As in the drawing room, new panelling in MDF has been added, here up to dado level. The plain modern divan has been given an air of contemporary luxury with the addition of a quilted satin bedhead.**

*RIGHT* **Two major architectural alterations were made to the house in the 19th century: the windows were modernized to incorporate the larger sheets of glass that were newly available, and an extra bay was added in the space at the side of the house where carriages once passed through to stables behind. On the first and second floors, this extra room has been used as a bathroom, here as an en suite leading off the main bedroom. Large contemporary flower paintings bring this room furnished with elegant antiques right up to date.**

The raised ground floor of the entrance hall was the obvious location for a drawing room, which spans the rear elevation overlooking the garden. New panelling in keeping with the period of the house now lines the room, and a pair of simple chimney pieces, also new, face each other from either end. It would take an expert eye to recognize that none of these architectural features is more than a few years old. Furnished with a comfortable mix of antiques and a subtly striped carpet laid over dark, polished boards, the style is relaxed and informal, more country vicarage than city townhouse.

Upstairs there is a capacious main bedroom with further fake panelling, in this instance to dado level, and a connecting bathroom contained in the extra room so conveniently provided by the Victorian extension. On the top floor there are two further bedrooms and another bathroom.

This is a clever restoration mainly because it is largely invisible. All traces of the house's more recent use as a clinic have disappeared so completely that it is now impossible to imagine it was ever anything other than the comfortable home it was built to be.

*ABOVE and LEFT* The ceiling beam behind the sofa marks the position of the wall that would once have divided the entrance hall from the living room. The removal of this wall at some stage before the house was listed makes the living room considerably bigger. The narrow wooden staircase is boxed in, a way of minimizing draughts before the days of central heating, and leads straight up from the living room.

# making your mark

*LEFT* The house is Tudor but the panelling in the living room probably dates from the 18th century, when the original fireplace, its width marked out by the eight-foot (two-and-a-half-metre) mantelpiece, was bricked in to make a smaller aperture flanked by cupboards. The lower mantelshelf looks as though it might be a 19th-century addition. Houses as old as this tend to have layers of architectural additions, in this instance unified by a single paint colour, Farrow & Ball's Old White.

*A timber-framed wattle and daub cottage dating from the 16th century is a rare survival in suburban London. Fiona and Martin Woodhouse's cottage sits in a terrace yards from the River Thames, built as a dormitory to house craftsmen working on Hampton Court Palace. With its steeply pitched roof and weatherboarded facade, it looks as though it belongs in a fishing village rather than on the edge of a huge city.*

Fiona and Martin run a design partnership from home specializing in corporate brochures and literature. They share a passion for interiors and a taste for the muted colours, faded gilding, and distressed paintwork of French and Swedish decorative antiques. Far from being discouraged by the fact that the house was unrestored and shabby, they appreciated its eccentricities.

'We decided to work with the building rather than strip away its quirky details,' says Martin. 'There are lots of odd features, added over the years – bits of wood banged into the panelling where someone once hung a picture, a funny drawer that pulls out from under the stairs, a fireplace that has been turned into a cupboard. All the floors slope, the beams sag, and none of the walls are straight, but we love that sense of history. It's as if everyone who has lived here has somehow left their mark.'

While being at pains not to wipe away these traces of the past, Fiona and Martin have gently imprinted their own 21st-century mark on the

house. Most of their changes are skin-deep, a question of painting the ancient wooden panelling downstairs and walls upstairs in their favoured off-whites and pale greys. In the dining room they installed a plain Victorian corner chimney piece, having found an old fireplace hidden by cupboards, and in the second bedroom they added a washbasin, cunningly housed in a battered wooden cabinet.

Only the little kitchen, which leads from the dining room, required more radical treatment. Here they removed an ugly partition, which separated it from a 1970s 'sunroom' at the back of the house. They lined the old kitchen walls with tongue-and-groove panelling, giving it the feel of a neat ship's cabin and conveniently disguising untidy pipes, and they added glazing bars to the windows of the extension to make them fit more comfortably with the period feel of the rest of the house.

The tongue and groove works well as a transition from the very old part of the house to

*RIGHT* In the 1970s a 'sunroom' was built at the back of the house. By taking down the partition that divided it from the tiny kitchen, and by adding the only radiator in the house and upgrading the windows, Fiona and Martin have incorporated it as extra kitchen space and home office.

*FAR RIGHT* The extension also houses essential storage, including fitted cupboards for the glass and crockery it was hard to find space for in the kitchen.

*OPPOSITE and THIS PICTURE* The dining room leads off the main living room and through to the kitchen, and is surprisingly bright with its tall window overlooking the back garden. Fiona and Martin added a small 19th-century corner fireplace where an original fireplace had been blocked in, and Martin made the table using reclaimed planks. One of his paintings, in the house palette of greys, browns, and off-whites, hangs above the sideboard under the slope of the stairs.

its most recent addition, and the former sunroom
feels more integrated as a result. A cottage of this
date would not have had a dedicated kitchen but,
thanks to the 1970s extension, Fiona and Martin
have been able to create the light, spacious feel
we now prefer for a room that is so well used.
The extra space also doubles as a home office.

Other changes made by past owners have been
similarly helpful. When the cottage was built the
living room would have been separated from a
narrow hallway by a wooden screen. At some
stage someone removed this old partition wall so
that the room now spans the width of the cottage.
Upstairs the low ceilings, which could have made
the space feel cramped and claustrophobic, have
been taken out so that the rooms now rise into
the beamed apex of the roof.

This opening out of rooms that to modern
sensibilities would seem too small means that a
Tudor workman's home can still be comfortable
and practical today. Thanks to another addition,
a two-storey lean-to, there is even space for
lavatories and baths. There is, however, only one
radiator in the whole house, under the windows
in the kitchen extension. This is supplemented by
a couple of night storage heaters. 'We didn't want
to start ripping up the old floorboards to put
heating in,' Martin explains. 'A fire, and being
insulated by the wood panelling, keeps us warm.'
Just as it did four hundred and fifty years ago.

French country-house style characterizes the main bedroom, with its French bed topped by a gilded wooden frame and dressed in an antique quilt. There is hardly room for bedside tables, so wall brackets, painted to match the walls, hold the pair of glass lamps and the alarm clock. Here, and elsewhere in the house, mirrors are used to increase the impression of space. The planked doors with their country latches help to give the room its rustic charm.

# country house furniture and lighting

Traditionally, and for those who could afford it, the country house was a retreat from the crowds and commerce, the noise and excitement of city life. Here you sought relaxation, as you entertained your friends or shot wildlife for sport. This is the role fulfilled by today's weekend cottage or pop-star-style manor — houses that promise rest and recuperation, with a log fire to curl up beside after a bracing walk or a shady garden arbour for a nap on a hot summer's afternoon.

Most of us do not own second houses, and most of us choose to live where we work, in or near a city. But country-house style can work just as well in a city street or a suburb as in the middle of fields. Designer Helen Ellery decorated her tiny London home as a retreat from city life within the city, using country-house style to evoke her rural childhood. Belinda and Adrian Hull's inner-city home has the genteel atmosphere of a country rectory. Like all 'styles' of decoration, country-house style can be applied almost anywhere. At its most successful it is a way of decorating and furnishing your home that offers comfort, relaxation and escapism, even if you are only a bus stop away from the office.

BIG PIECES of furniture have the right generosity of scale. Oddly, you can make a small room seem bigger with an oversized sofa, as in Helen Ellery's sitting room. In the same way, a four-poster bed bestows grandeur on a poky bedroom.

THE OLD-FASHIONED country house is always furnished with a mix of pieces from different periods, acquisitions gradually added over generations. The effect is of rooms that have 'grown' as opposed to rooms that have been 'decorated'. To achieve this organic look you need to shop around and be patient. Don't be in a rush to get it right immediately.

ANTIQUES ARE IMPORTANT for the country-house look and give a room a sense of history. It is better to save up for a couple of good pieces than blow the budget on lesser stuff.

BIG IS BETTER for lamps as well as furniture. Small table lamps look feeble. Check the proportion of the shade by measuring its widest diameter against the height of the stand. The two should be about equal.

BEEF UP a plain metal chandelier by adding greenery or branches, as in the Lothons' breakfast room.

THINK DOGS AND CHILDREN even if you don't have either. For an interior to feel truly relaxing it needs to have been knocked about a little bit. If dogs or children would be a threat to its perfection, it must be too smart for comfort.

COMFORT is probably the single most important design ingredient of this style. Sit, lie, and curl up on a sofa before you consider buying it for its good looks.

FOR INSTANT country-house credibility in the kitchen you can't beat an Aga. However, Agas are fiendishly expensive and monumentally heavy. If you can't afford an Aga you might be able to afford a ceramic Belfast sink — that other icon of the country kitchen.

IF YOUR KITCHEN is big enough, consider making space for a sofa. This instantly transforms it into that estate agents' legend, a 'farmhouse kitchen', and, jargon aside, makes it feel like a room for lying around in, not just for peeling potatoes.

NO COUNTRY-HOUSE interior would be complete without a fire. Apple-wood logs are the ideal but a gas-effect fire is sufficiently realistic and agreeably low maintenance. A fire in the bedroom or bathroom is a particularly delicious indulgence.

# country house fabric and finishing touches

One of the key features of country-house style is comfort, and fabrics are one of the key means of providing it. Because the tone of these interiors is so relaxed you can have fun with fabrics, mixing patterns, piling up cushions, layering bed linen and quilts, and throwing throws wherever you think you might need the warmth of a lap blanket or shawl.

The effect you want is one of effortless informality, as if you have inherited the curtains, made the cushions out of an old dress, and bought the sofas at auction and kept their original covers. And somehow, miraculously, it all goes together. Needless to say, it is never as simple as that. Mixing different patterns successfully is far more difficult than sticking to safe cream and taupe. As is often the case, trial and error will get you there in the end.

Exactly the same principle applies to finishing touches, which are less essential to comfort but equally pertinent to the finished effect. Country-house style allows you to indulge in some restrained clutter. Pictures can be traditional or contemporary. Dark, gilt-framed oil paintings add richness to the interiors of the Lothons' French farmhouse, while the bright, bold contemporary flower paintings in the Hulls' bedroom make splashes of fresh modernity in a room furnished with antiques.

**CHINTZ is the quintessential country-house fabric, blowsy with bouquets of garden flowers, traditional, English and pretty. For a dramatic and surprisingly sophisticated effect in a bedroom, use it to excess, with matching curtains, wallpaper, bedcover and upholstery.**

**FADED CHINTZ is even more quintessential. Some of the most upmarket fabric houses produce designs in nicotine-stained colours that already look as though they have been hanging for generations. Or you can take the more taxing route and try dyeing a brash new chintz with a strong solution of tea.**

**SECOND-HAND OR ANTIQUE curtains may save on tea. It doesn't matter if they are too long; they can 'puddle' on the floor. It does matter if they are too short, although you can always add a border to their bottoms in a co-ordinating colour.**

**SHORT CURTAINS that reach just below the window sill look cottagey. Long curtains that sit on the floor are more in tune with this style.**

FABRIC can be stretched on a framework of battens to line a room instead of wallpaper, giving an effect that is deeply luxurious.

LOOSE COVERS have a more relaxed, informal feel than fitted upholstery and can be whipped off and washed when the smell of wet Labrador becomes overpowering.

LOOK OUT FOR antique table linen — it is very good value. Any old table is transformed when hidden under the heavy folds of a good-quality damask cloth. Add a set of napkins, large enough to envelop your lap, and you will feel you are dining in stately splendour.

DON'T BANISH BOOKS to the downstairs cloakroom or a dark corridor. A full bookcase adds depth, colour and texture to any room, not to mention providing an endless source of interest and entertainment.

GLASS-FRONTED cabinets, whether painted country-kitchen style or polished mahogany, are the perfect storage for small, decorative items, at once showing them off and keeping them safe and dust-free.

# UK directory

## FURNITURE

### George Smith
587–589 King's Road
London SW6 2EH
020 7384 1004
www.georgesmith.co.uk
*Capacious and relaxed traditional sofas and armchairs.*

### Habitat
08444 991111 for your nearest branch
www.habitat.net
*Accessible contemporary furnishings at accessible prices, plus remakes of classic 20th-century designs including sofas and armchairs by Robin Day.*

### Josephine Ryan Antiques
63 Abbeville Road
London SW4 9JW
020 8675 3900
www.josephineryan antiques.co.uk
*A dealer with her finger on the fashion pulse.*

### Knoll International
1 Lindsey Street
East Market
London EC1A 9PQ
020 7236 6655
www.knoll-english.com
*Design classics by Florence Knoll, Saarinen, Breuer, Frank Gehry and Mies van der Rohe.*

### Nordic Style
109 Lots Road
London SW10 0RN
020 7351 1755
www.nordicstyle.com
*Furniture, accessories and fabrics inspired by Swedish Gustavian originals.*

## FINISHING TOUCHES

### Carden Cunietti
1A Adpar Street
London W2 1DE
020 7724 9679
www.carden-cunietti.com
*Beautiful glass and other desirable accessories, quirky and glamorous.*

### Graham & Green
4 Elgin Crescent
London W11 2HX
020 7243 8908
www.grahamand green.co.uk
*Glamorous glass, cushions, tableware; some furniture, including leather items.*

### Paul Young
Station Pottery
Shenton Lane
Shenton, Nuneaton
Warwickshire CV13 0AA
07711 628337
*Traditional slipware pottery, highly decorative and eminently useable.*

### Roger Oates
Studio and shop:
The Long Barn
Eastnor, Ledbury
Herefordshire HR8 1EL
01531 632718
www.rogeroates.com
*All kinds of natural floorings including chunky abaca, flat-weave rugs and runners in subtle stripes, felt matting.*

## FABRICS

### Bennison Fabrics
16 Holbein Place
London SW1W 8NL
020 7730 8076
www.bennisonfabrics.com
*Chintzes that already look as though they have been dipped in tea to save you the trouble of doing it yourself.*

### Chelsea Textiles
13 Walton Street
London SW3 2HX
020 7584 5544
www.chelseatextiles.com
*Embroidered cottons, linens, silks and voiles with an 18th-century feel.*

### Colefax and Fowler
39 Brook Street
London W1K 4JE
020 7493 2231

110 Fulham Road
London SW3 6HU
020 7244 7427
www.colefaxantiques.com
*Unbeatable for English fabrics, chintz and wallpapers.*

### Ian Mankin
109 Regent's Park Road
London NW1 8UR
020 7722 0997
www.ianmankin.com
*Huge range of natural fabrics, including unbleached linens, butter muslin and striped tickings.*

### Pavilion Antiques
Bradford-on-Avon
01225 866136 for an appointment
*Dealer in antique French linens, sheeting, mattress tickings and curtains.*

## KITCHENS

### Aga Rayburn
08457 125207
www.agarayburn.co.uk
*Classic cast-iron heat storage cookers, essential for country kitchens, even in town.*

### Bulthaup
37 Wigmore Street
London W1U 1PP
020 7495 3663
www.bulthaup.com
*Contemporary and high-tech kitchens, high quality and clever design.*

### Divertimenti
227–229 Brompton Road
London SW3 2EP
020 7581 8065
www.divertimenti.co.uk
*Complete range of cookware and kitchen accessories.*

### Plain English Kitchen Design
Stowupland Hall
Stowupland, Stowmarket
Suffolk IP14 4BE
0870 2403562 for brochure
www.plainenglish design.co.uk
*Well-designed wooden kitchens suitable for period and traditional interiors.*

## BATHROOMS

### Antique Bathrooms of Ivybridge
Erme Bridge Works
Ermington Road, Ivybridge
Devon PL21 9DE
01752 698250
www.antiquebaths.com
*Reconditioned antique baths and sanitary ware, plus reproduction ranges.*

### C. P. Hart
Newnham Terrace
Hercules Road
London SE1 7DR
020 7902 5250
and branches
www.cphart.co.uk
*Inspiring showrooms for kitchens as well as bathrooms with bathroom designs by Philippe Starck among others.*

### Sitting Pretty
Preston Farm Court
Lower Road
Little Bookham
Surrey KT23 4EF
020 7381 0049
www.sittingpretty bathrooms.co.uk
*Classical bathroom suites and accessories.*

### Stiffkey Bathrooms
89 Upper St Giles Street
Norwich NR2 1AB
01603 627850
www.stiffkeybath rooms.com
*Antique sanitary ware and own range of period bathroom accessories.*

## PAINT AND PAPER

### Farrow & Ball
Uddens Estate
Wimborne
Dorset BH21 7NL
01202 876141 for stockists
www.farrow-ball.com
*Unbeatable for subtle paint colours with strange names, also papers, varnishes and stains.*

### de Gournay
112 Old Church Street
London SW3 6EP
020 7352 9988
www.degournay.com
*Reproductions of 18th-century Chinese wallpapers and early 19th-century French scenic wallpapers.*

### Lewis & Wood
Woodchester Mill
North Woodchester
Stroud
Gloucestershire GL5 5NN
01453 878517
www.lewisandwood.co.uk
*Interesting and eccentric wallpapers including old-fashioned hunting, fishing and golfing scenes. Also toiles, linens and desirable linen velvets and chenilles.*

### The Paint Library
5 Elystan Street
London SW3 3NT
020 7823 7755
www.paintlibrary.co.uk
*Excellent quality paint and wallpaper, including innumerable shades of off-white.*

### Papers and Paints
4 Park Walk
London SW10 0AD
020 7352 8626
www.papers-paints.co.uk
*Own excellent range of paints, and they will mix any colour to order.*

### Sanderson
01895 830000 for stockists
www.sanderson-uk.com
*Original wallpapers designed by William Morris, some also available as hand-blocked prints.*

## LIGHTING

### Charles Edwards
582 King's Road
London SW6 2DY
020 7736 8490
www.charlesedwards.com
*High-quality reproduction lighting, with an especially good selection of lanterns.*

### John Cullen Lighting
585 King's Road
London SW6 2EH
020 7371 5400
www.johncullen lighting.co.uk
*Extensive range of contemporary light fittings and a bespoke lighting design service.*

### Vaughan
G1, Chelsea Harbour
Design Centre
Chelsea Harbour
London SW10 0XE
020 7349 4600
www.vaughandesigns.com
*Comprehensive range of replica period lighting from lamps to sconces to chandeliers.*

# US directory

## FURNITURE

### Brimfield Antique Show
Route 20
Brimfield, MA 01010
(413) 245-3436
www.brimfieldshow.com
*This famous flea market runs for a week in May, July, and September. For listings of other flea markets around the country, visit www.fleamarket.com.*

### Charles P. Rogers
55 West Seventeenth Street
New York, NY 10011
(212) 675-4400
www.charlesprogers.com
*Brass, iron, and wood bed frames.*

### Crate & Barrel
646 N. Michigan Avenue
Chicago, IL 60611
and stores nationwide
Call (800) 967-6696 for
a retail outlet near you.
www.crateandbarrel.com
*Contemporary furniture and accessories for every room.*

### Ethan Allen
Check the website for
a retail outlet near you.
www.ethanallen.com
*Classic furniture for every room of the home.*

### Country French Interiors
1428 Slocum Street
Dallas, TX 75207
(214) 747-4700
www.countryfrench
    interiors.com
*18th- and 19th-century French antiques.*

### Herman Miller Inc.
855 East Main Avenue
Zeeland, MI 49464-0302
(616) 654-3000
www.hermanmiller.com
*Furniture by Alvar Aalto and other fine 20th-century furniture designers.*

### Jane Keltner Collections
Brighton Pavilion
Memphis, TN 38117
(800) 487-8033
www.janekeltner.com
*Painted furniture and antique reproductions.*

### Pottery Barn
100–104 Seventh Avenue
New York, NY 10011
Call (888) 779-5176 for
a retail outlet near you.
www.potterybarn.com
*Contemporary furniture and accessories for the home.*

### Shaker Style Furnishings
292 Chesham Road
Harrisville, NH 03450
(888) 824-3340
www.shakerstyle.com
*Custom-built Shaker-style furniture and home accents.*

### Swartzendruber Hardwood Creations
1100 Chicago Avenue
Goshen, IN 46528
(800) 531-2502
www.swartzendruber.com
*Mission, Shaker, and Prairie-style quality reproductions.*

## FINISHING TOUCHES

### ABC Carpet & Home
888 Broadway
New York, NY 10003
(212) 473-3000
www.abchome.com
*Accessories for the home representing all periods and styles.*

### Anthropologie
1801 Walnut Street
Philadelphia, PA 19103
(215) 568-2114
www.anthropologie.com
*Vintage-inspired one-of-a-kind decorative details.*

### Moss
150 Greene Street
New York, NY 10012
(866) 888-6677
www.mossonline.com
*Original and reproduction American decorative objects.*

### Williamsburg Marketplace
(800) 446-9240
www.williamsburgmarket
    place.com
*Reproductions of Colonial pewter, prints, and other decorative accessories.*

## FABRICS

### Clarence House
979 Third Avenue, Suite 205
New York, NY 10022
(212) 752-2890
www.clarencehouse.com
*Natural-fiber fabrics with prints based on 15th- to 20th-century patterns. Also fine wallpapers.*

### Peter Fasano
964 Main Street
Great Barrington,
MA 01230
(413) 528-6872
www.peterfasano.com
*Hand-painted fabric and wallpaper designs.*

### Pierre Deux
979 Third Avenue,
Suite 134
New York, NY 10022
(212) 644-4891
www.pierredeux.com
*French country fabric, upholstery, wallpaper, and antiques.*

### Smith + Noble
(800) 248-8888
www.smithandnoble.com
*Window treatments of all kinds plus fabric by the yard.*

### Thibaut
480 Frelinghuysen Avenue
Newark, NJ 07114
(800) 223-0704
www.thibautdesign.com
*Textile dealer specializing in wallpaper.*

## KITCHENS

### Bosch
Visit the website to find
a showroom near you.
www.boschappliances.com
*Quality kitchen appliances and fixtures.*

### Crown Point Cabinetry
PO Box 1560
Claremont, NH 03743
(800) 999-4994
www.crown-point.com
*Custom cabinets for kitchen and bath.*

### Harrington Brassworks
(201) 818-1300
www.harrington
    brassworks.com
*Brass faucets for kitchen and bath in classic styles.*

### Paris Ceramics
150 East 58th Street,
7th Floor
New York, NY 10155
(212) 644-2782
www.parisceramics.com
*Limestone, terracotta, antique stone, and hand-painted tiles.*

### Poggenpohl
Visit the website to find
a showroom near you.
www.poggenpohl-usa.com
*Specializes in customized kitchen designs.*

### Quintessentials
532 Amsterdam Avenue
New York, NY 10024
(212) 877-1919 or
(888) 676-BATH
www.qkb.com
*Quality kitchen cabinets, appliances, hardware, and accessories.*

### Stone Panels
100 South Royal Lane
Coppell, TX 75019
(800) 328-6275
www.stonepanels.com
*Stone surfaces, from limestone to granite to marble.*

## BATHROOMS

### Antique Hardware & Home
421 East Norway
Mitchell, SD 57301
(877) 823-7567
www.antiquehardware.com
*Unusual and antique hardware and fixtures.*

### Kallista
Visit the website to find
a showroom near you.
(888) 4-KALLISTA
www.kallistainc.com
*Mahogany tub surrounds, sleek and modern fixtures, and much more.*

### Kohler
Visit the website to find
a showroom near you.
(800) 456-4537
www.kohlerco.com
*Wide range of bathtub, sink, and bathroom accessories.*

### Signature Hardware
2700 Crescent Springs Pike
Erlanger, KY 41017
(866) 855-2284
www.signature
    hardware.com
*Authentic reproduction clawfoot tubs, pedestal and console sinks, Topaz copper soaking tubs, and more.*

### Vintage Plumbing
9645 Sylvia Avenue
Northridge, CA 91324
(818) 772-1721
www.vintageplumbing.com
*Original and restored bathroom antiques, including pull-chain toilets and clawfoot bathtubs.*

### Waterworks
60 Backus Avenue
Danbury, CT 06810
(800) 927-2120
www.waterworks.com
*Bathroom fixtures, cabinets, lighting, and fittings.*

### Wonder Shower
16920 Kuykendahl,
Suite 218
Houston, TX 77068
(800) 595-0385
www.showeringgifts.com
*Showerheads in brushed nickel, brass, copper, platinum, chrome, in sloping, extension, or dual-arm designs.*

## LIGHTING

### Eron Johnson Antiques
451 North Broadway
Denver, CO 80203
(303) 777-8700
www.eronjohnson
    antiques.com
*Antique table lamps, wall sconces, candelabra, chandeliers, and more.*

### R 20th Century Design
82 Franklin Street
New York, NY 10013
(212) 343-7979
www.r20thcentury.com
*Includes mid-century modern lamps and lighting fixtures.*

### Van Dyke's Restorers
421 East Norway
Mitchell, SD 57301
(800) 787-3355
www.vandykes.com
*Restored lighting fixtures from Victorian to Art Deco to Mission style.*

# picture credits

The publishers would like to thank all those who allowed us to photograph their homes for this book.

Photography by Christopher Drake unless stated otherwise    KEY: *ph*=photographer, a=above, b=below, r=right, l=left, c=centre

Endpapers *ph* Ray Main; 1 the home of Cosmo Fry and Lulu Anderson; 2 designer Stephen Pardy's Georgian house in London; 3 Fiona and Woody Woodhouse's 16th-century weatherboard cottage in Surrey designed by Bexon Woodhouse Creative; 4–5 *ph* Ray Main / Central London apartment designed by Ben Kelly Design, 1999; 6 the home of Adrian and Belinda Hull in London designed by architect Gus Alexander; 8 textile designer Neisha Crosland's London home / furnishing, fabrics and wallpapers in Chelsea Green – Ginka clothes collection on Fulham Road; 9–11 Fiona and Woody Woodhouse's 16th-century weatherboard cottage in Surrey designed by Bexon Woodhouse Creative; 12–19 designer Stephen Pardy's Georgian house in London; 20–25 Tim Whittaker's Georgian house in East London; 26–29 *ph* Chris Everard / Eric De Queker's apartment in Antwerp; 30–33 *ph* Jan Baldwin / interior designer Philip Hooper's own house in East Sussex; 34a *ph* Andrew Wood; 34bl a house in Salisbury designed by Helen Ellery of The Plot London; 34br designer Stephen Pardy's Georgian house in London; 35a & bl *ph* Jan Baldwin / Christopher Leach's apartment in London; 35bc a house in Salisbury designed by Helen Ellery of The Plot London; 35br *ph* Andrew Wood; 36al *ph* Alan Williams / the Norfolk home of Geoff and Gilly Newberry of Bennison Fabrics – curtain fabric Malabar by Bennison; 36ar & br *ph* Jan Baldwin; 36bl & 37l *ph* Andrew Wood; 37ar the home of Adrian and Belinda Hull in London designed by architect Gus Alexander; 37bc Tim Whittaker's Georgian house in East London; 37br *ph* Alan Williams / the Norfolk home of Geoff and Gilly Newberry of Bennison Fabrics – cushion and sofa fabric Tokyo Rose on beige linen by Bennison; 38–39 *ph* Chris Everard / an apartment in Paris designed by architect Paul Collier; 40–45 *ph* Fritz von der Schulenburg / Frédéric Méchiche's apartment in Paris; 46–49 *ph* Chris Everard / an apartment in Paris designed by architect Paul Collier; 50–55 *ph* Jan Baldwin / the New York home of Gael Towey, Creative Director of Martha Stewart Living Omnimedia and Stephen Doyle, Creative Director of Doyle Partners; 56–61 *ph* Jan Baldwin / interior designer Timothy Whealon's Manhattan apartment; 62–67 antique dealer and co-owner of Jamb Ltd / antique chimney pieces; 68–73 textile designer Neisha Crosland's London home / furnishing, fabrics and wallpapers in Chelsea Green – Ginka clothes collection on Fulham Road; 74al & b *ph* Chris Everard / an apartment in Milan designed by Daniela Micol Wajskol, interior designer; 74ar–75al *ph* Tom Leighton / Keith Varty and Alan Cleaver's apartment in London designed by Jonathan Reed/Reed Boyd (now Studio Reed); 75ar *ph* Andrew Wood / Jane Collins of Sixty 6 in Marylebone High Street, home in Central London; 75bc Valentina Albini's home in Milan; 76l *ph* Polly Wreford / Ros Fairman's house in London; 76c *ph* Tom Leighton / Keith Varty and Alan Cleaver's apartment in London designed by Jonathan Reed/Reed Boyd (now Studio Reed); 76r–77l *ph* Verity Welstead / Lulu Guinness' house in London; 77c *ph* Jan Baldwin / David Gill's house in London; 77r *ph* Chris Everard; 78–79 a country house in the Luberon, Provence with interior design by François Gilles and Dominique Lubar of IPL Interiors and Pierre-Marie Gilles – Paris; 80–85 *ph* Jan Baldwin / Michael D'Souza of Mufti; 86–91 a country house in the Luberon, Provence with interior design by François Gilles and Dominique Lubar of IPL Interiors and Pierre-Marie Gilles – Paris; 92–97 *ph* Ray Main / Marina and Peter Hill's barn in West Sussex designed by Marina Hill; Peter James Construction Management, Chichester; The West Sussex Antique Timber Company, Wisborough Green; and Joanna Jefferson Architects; 98–101 Diana Boston of The Manor, Hemingford Grey, Cambs – available for tours t. 01480 463134; 102a *ph* Tom Leighton; 102bl *ph* James Merrell; 102br *ph* Chris Tubbs / Daniel Jasiak's home near Biarritz; 103al–r *ph* James Merrell / Richard Spizzirri and Holly Leuders' house in Aspen; 103c & br *ph* Chris Tubbs; 103bl *ph* Ray Main; 104ar *ph* Chris Tubbs / Jenny Makepeace's house in Dorset; 104bl *ph* James Merrell / design by Jim Ruscitto, architect; 105al a country house in the Luberon, Provence with interior design by François Gilles and Dominique Lubar of IPL Interiors and Pierre-Marie Gilles – Paris; 105ar *ph* Polly Wreford / Ann Shore's house in London; 105b *ph* Chris Tubbs / Phil Lapworth's tree house near Bath; 106–107 *ph* Ray Main / Jonathan Leitersdorf's apartment in New York designed by Jonathan Leitersdorf/Just Design Ltd; 108–113 *ph* Ray Main / Evan Snyderman's house in Brooklyn; 114–119 *ph* Ray Main / Jonathan Leitersdorf's apartment in New York designed by Jonathan Leitersdorf/Just Design Ltd; 120–125 *ph* Ray Main / client's residence, East Hampton, New York designed by ZG DESIGN; 126–131 *ph* Ray Main / Kenneth Hirst's apartment in New York; 132–137 *ph* Ray Main / Central London apartment designed by Ben Kelly Design, 1999; 138–143 *ph* Jan Baldwin / interior designer/stylist Mark Smith's house in Gloucestershire; 144l *ph* Ray Main; 144r *ph* Jan Baldwin / interior architect Joseph Dirand's apartment in Paris; 145al *ph* Tom Leighton; 145ac *ph* Ray Main; 145ar *ph* Polly Wreford; 145b *ph* Ray Main / Alastair Gordon and Barbara de Vries' house near Princeton designed by Smith-Miller + Hawkinson Architects; 146al *ph* Ray Main / Greville and Sophie Worthington's home in Yorkshire; 146r *ph* Alan Williams / Juan Corbella's apartment in London designed by HM2, Richard Webb with Andrew Hanson; 146bl *ph* Catherine Gratwicke / Jonathan Adler and Simon Doonan's apartment in New York; 147bl *ph* Catherine Gratwicke / Kari Sigerson's apartment in New York; 147c *ph* Ray Main / a house in Paris designed by Hervé Vermesch; 147r *ph* Catherine Gratwicke / Renée Syner, New York; 148–149 the home of Cosmo Fry and Lulu Anderson; 150–155 owners of La Cour Beaudeval Antiquities, Mireille and Jean-Claude Lothon's house in Faverolles; 156–161 *ph* Chris Everard / a house in London designed by Helen Ellery of The Plot London, paintings by Robert Clarke; 162–169 the home of Cosmo Fry and Lulu Anderson; 170–175 the home of Adrian and Belinda Hull in London designed by architect Gus Alexander; 176–181 Fiona and Woody Woodhouse's 16th-century weatherboard cottage in Surrey designed by Bexon Woodhouse Creative; 182al & 183br *ph* Alan Williams / the Arbuthnott family's house near Cirencester designed by Nicholas Arbuthnott, fabrics designed by Vanessa Arbuthnott; 182ar, b & 183ac Vivien Lawrence, an interior designer in London t. 020 8209 0562; 183bl & 184 *ph* Tom Leighton / Roger and Fay Oates' house in Ledbury; 185al *ph* Alan Williams / the Norfolk home of Geoff and Gilly Newberry of Bennison Fabrics – walls, Daisy Chain on oyster by Bennison; 185b Vivien Lawrence, an interior designer in London t. 020 8209 0562; 185r a country house in the Luberon, Provence with interior design by François Gilles and Dominique Lubar of IPL Interiors and Pierre-Marie Gilles – Paris.

## architects and designers whose work is featured in this book

**Ann Shore**
London-based designer and stylist, owner of Story: personal selection of old and new furniture and accessories. Appointment only.
t. 020 7377 0313
*Page 105ar*

**Ben Kelly Design**
10 Stoney Street
London SE1 9AD
t. 020 7378 8116
ben@bkduk.co.uk
www.benkellydesign.com
*Pages 4–5, 132–137*

**Bennison Fabrics**
16 Holbein Place
London SW1W 9NL
t. 020 7730 8076
bennisonfabrics@
  btinternet.com
www.bennisonfabrics.com

U.S.
The Fine Arts Building
232 East 59th Street
New York, NY 10022
t. +1 212 223 0373
*Pages 36al, 37br, 185al*

**Bernard M. Wharton**
Shope Reno Wharton Associates
18 West Putnam Avenue
Greenwich CT 06830
USA
t. +1 203 869 7250
j.hupy@srwol.com
www.shoprenowharton.com
*Page 102br*

**Bexon Woodhouse Creative**
t. 01531 630176
www.bexonwoodhouse.com
*Pages 3, 11, 176–181*

**Christopher Leach**
Interior Designer
m. 07765 255666
mail@christopherleach.com
*Page 35a & bl*

**Cosmo Fry**
The Big Sleep Hotel
Bute Terrace
Cardiff CF10 2FE
t. 02920 636363
www.bigsleephotel.com
*Pages 1, 76r–77l, 148–149, 162–169*

**Diana Boston**
The Manor
Hemingford Grey
Cambs PE28 9BN
t. 01480 463134
diana_boston@hotmail.com
www.greenknowe.co.uk
*Pages 98–101*

**Dirand Joseph Architecture**
338 rue des Pyrénées
75020 Paris
France
t. +33 01 47 97 78 57
joseph.dirand@wanadoo.fr
*Page 144r*

**Eric De Queker**
Koninklijkelaan 44
2600 Berchem
Belgium
eric.de.queker@pandora.be
*Pages 26–29*

**Gus Alexander Architects**
46–47 Britton Street
London EC1M 5UJ
t. 020 7336 7227
gusalex@btinternet.com
www.gusalexander
architects.com
*Pages 6, 37ar, 170–175*

**Helen Ellery**
The Plot London,
Interior Design
73 Compton Street
London EC1V 0BN
t. 07974 173026
helen@helenellery.com
*Pages 34bl, 35bc, 156–161*

**Hervé Vermesch**
Architect
50 rue Richat
75010 Paris
France
t. +33 1 42 01 39 39
*Page 147c*

**Hirst Pacific Ltd**
250 Lafayette Street
New York, NY 10012
USA
t. +1 212 625 3670
kennethhirst@hirst
pacific.com
www.hirstpacific.com
*Pages 126–131*

**HM2 Architects**
Richard Webb,
Project Director
Andrew Hanson, Director
33–37 Charterhouse Square
London EC1M 6EA
t. 020 7600 5151
andrew.hanson@
harper-mackay.co.uk
*Page 146r*

**Holly Leuders Design**
Building, interior and
furniture design
27 West 67th Street
New York, NY 10023
USA
t. +1 212 787 9485
*Page 103al–r*

**IPL Interiors**
25 Bullen Street
London SW11 3ER
t. 020 7978 4224
*Pages 78–79, 86–91, 105al,
185r*
Also for this project:
Pierre-Marie Gilles, Paris
t. +33 1 46 04 82 49

**Garrett Finney**
FARO
1207 Arlington Street
Houston, TX 77008
USA
t. +1 713 303 3862
garrettfinney@earthlink.net
*Pages 78–79, 86–91, 105al,
185r*

**Jamb Limited**
Antique chimney pieces.
Core One, The Gas Works
Gate D, Michael Road
London SW6 2AN
t. 020 7736 3006
sales@jamblimited.com
www.jamblimited.com
*Pages 62–67*

**Jim Ruscitto, Architect**
P.O. Box 419
Sun Valley, IO 83353
USA
t. +1 208 726 1033
*Page 104bl*

**Joanna Jefferson Architects**
222 Oving Road
Chichester
West Sussex PO19 4EJ
t. 01243 532 398
jjeffearch@aol.com
*Pages 92–97*

**Jonathan Adler**
465 Broome Street
New York, NY 10013
USA
t. +1 212 941 8950
www.jonathanadler.com
*Page 146bl*

**Jonathan Leitersdorf**
Just Design
80 Fifth Avenue, 18th Floor
New York, NY 10011
USA
t. +1 212 243 6544
*Pages 106–107, 114–119*

**Mireille and Jean-Claude
Lothon**
La Cour Beaudeval
Antiquites
4 rue des Fontaines
28210 Faverolles
France
t. +33 2 37 51 47 67
*Pages 150–155*

**Lulu Anderson**
Lulu at Babington House
near Frome
Somerset BA11 3RW
t. 01373 812653
*Pages 1, 76r–77l, 148–149,
162–169*

**Lulu Guinness**
3 Ellis Street
London SW1X 9AL
t. 020 7823 4828
www.luluguinness.com
*Pages 76r–77l*

**Mark Smith at Smithcreative**
15 St George's Road
London W4 1AU
t. 020 8747 3909
mark@smithcreative.net
*Pages 138–143*

**Frédéric Méchiche**
4 Rue de Thorigny
75003 Paris
France
*Pages 40–45*

**Mufti**
789 Fulham Road
London SW6 5HD
t. 020 7610 9123
Interior design:
interiors@mufti.co.uk
Bespoke furniture:
info@mufti.co.uk
www.mufti.co.uk
*Pages 80–85*

**Neisha Crosland**
8 Elystan Street
London SW3 3NS
t. 020 7584 7988

US Showroom:
22 West 56th Street, #3B
New York, NY 10019
USA
t. +1 212 397 8257
www.neishacrosland.com
*Pages 8, 68–73*

**Nicholas Arbuthnott**
Arbuthnott Ladenbury
Architects & Urban
Designers
15 Gosditch Street
Cirencester GL7 2AG
*Pages 182al, 183br*

**Paul Collier**
Architect
113 rue St Maur
75011 Paris
France
t. +33 1 53 72 49 32
paul.collier@architecte.net
*Pages 38–39, 46–49*

**Philip Hooper**
Colefax & Fowler
Decorating, antiques,
wallpapers and fabrics
118 Garratt Lane
London SW18 4DJ
t. 020 8874 6484
*Pages 30–33*

**Roger Oates Design**
Shop and Showroom:
1 Munro Terrace
(off Cheyne Walk)
London SW10 0DL

Studio Shop:
The Long Barn
Eastnor, Ledbury
Herefordshire HR8 1EL
Mail-order catalogue
t. 01531 631611
www.rogeroates.co.uk
*Pages 183bl, 184*

**Simon Kimmins Design and
Project Control**
t. 020 8314 1526
*Page 105b*

**Smith-Miller + Hawkinson
Architects LLP**
305 Canal Street, 4th Floor
New York, NY 10013
USA
t. +1 212 966 3875
contact@smharch.com
www.smharch.com
*Page 145b*

**Stephen Doyle**
Creative Director of
Doyle Partners
1123 Broadway at 25th Street
New York, NY 10010
USA
t. +1 212 463 8787
www.doylepartners.com
*Pages 50–55*

**Studio Reed (formerly Reed
Creative Services)**
151a Sydney Street
London SW3 6NT
t. 020 7565 0066
*Pages 74ar–75al*

**Timothy Whealon Inc**
23 East 69th Street, Apt 2
New York, NY 10021
USA
t. +1 212 249 2153
tjwhealon@tjwdesigns.com
www.timothywhealon.com
*Pages 56–61*

**Vanessa Arbuthnott Fabrics**
The Tallet, Calmsden
Cirencester GL7 5ET
www.vanessaarbuthnott.co.uk
*Pages 182al, 183br*

**Weston-Pardy Design
Consultancy**
t. 020 7587 0221
weston.pardy@mac.com
*Pages 2, 12–19, 34br*

**Zina Glazebrook**
ZG Design
P.O. Box 144
Sagaponack, NY 11962
USA
t. +1 631 324 1675
zina@zgdesign.com
www.zgdesign.com
*Pages 120–125*

ADDITIONAL
SUPPLIERS/
DESIGNERS/
STOCKISTS

**Alfie's Antiques Market**
13–25 Church Street
London NW8 8DT
t. 020 7723 6066

**Artwork**
Stephan Lacey Gallery
t. 020 7837 5507
Tim Pomeroy, Artist
Keith Rand, Artist
Rachel Schwalm, Artist
Sophie Smallhorn
Jonnie Delafield-Cooke
'Georgeous Macauley' painting
by Craigie Aitchison
Timothy Taylor Gallery
t. 020 7409 3344

**BROWNRIGG Interiors**
10a New Street
Petworth
West Sussex GU28 0AS
t. 01798 344321
info@brownrigg-interiors.com

**Chambre 19**
Decorative antiques.
26 Parsons Green Lane
London SW6 4HS
t. 020 7384 4538
jana@chambre19.com

**CF Design**
Kitchen accessories.
t. 01373 813582

**Countertops Bath**
t. 01225 424467

**DNA Design**
Core One, The Gas Works
2 Michael Road
London SW6 2AN
t. 020 7751 0022
xdnadesignx@aol.com

**Neisha Crosland**
Ginka
137 Fulham Road
London SW3 6SD
t. 020 7589 4866

**Jacobs Antiques**
West Canal Wharf
Cardiff CF10 5DB
t. 02920 390939

**James Townshend**
1970s lamp.
t. 01225 332290

**John Robbins Antiques**
t. 07710 609043

**Josephine Ryan**
Antiques and interiors.
63 Abbeville Road
London SW4 9JW
t. 020 8675 3900

**Julien Chichester Design**
t. 020 7622 2928

**Katherine Pole**
Antique textiles and
decorations.
t. 020 7286 5630

**Marius Barran**
Architect
t. 020 8960 7600

**Paint & Paper Library**
Showroom and Sampling:
5 Elystan Street
London SW3 3NT
t. 020 7581 1075
www.paintlibrary.co.uk

**Sean Walters**
The Plant Specialist
t. 07966 194575

**ShappacherWhite Ltd**
315 West 36th Street
Suite 1000
New York, NY 10018
USA
t. +1 212 279 1675

# index

Page numbers in *italic* refer to illustrations and their captions

# acknowledgments

The idea for this book was prompted by my own old house, which has been restored and conserved over the last two and a half years by an exceptional team of Devon craftsmen led by Dave Daines, including Ken Long, Brian Harris, Kevin Harris, Rodney Parsons and Derek Batten. Meanwhile, Jim Board has transformed the garden and Brenda Newton has fought valiantly against the dust.